THE SMALL GROUP LEADERS TRAINING COURSE

TRAINER'S MANUAL

DEVELOPED BY

DR. JUDY HAMLIN

NAVPRESS

A MINISTRY OF THE NAVIGATORS
P.O. BOX 35001, COLORADO SPRINGS, COLORADO 80935

The Navigators is an international Christian organization. Jesus Christ gave His followers the Great Commission to go and make disciples (Matthew 28:19). The aim of The Navigators is to help fulfill that commission by multiplying laborers for Christ in every nation.

NavPress is the publishing ministry of The Navigators. NavPress publications are tools to help Christians grow. Although publications alone cannot make disciples or change lives, they can help believers learn biblical discipleship, and apply what they learn to their lives and ministries.

Library of Congress Catalog Card Number: 90-61779
ISBN 08910-93087

Fourth printing, 1993

Interior illustrations: Darrell Skipworth

Unless otherwise noted, all Scripture quotations in this publication are from the *New American Standard Bible* (NASB), © The Lockman Foundation 1960, 1962, 1963, 1968, 1971, 1972, 1973, 1975, 1977. Other versions used are the *Amplified New Testament* (AMP), © The Lockman Foundation 1954, 1958; and the *Holy Bible: New International Version* (NIV). Copyright © 1973, 1978, 1984, International Bible Society. Used by permission of Zondervan Bible Publishers.

Printed in the United States of America

FOR A FREE CATALOG OF
NAVPRESS BOOKS & BIBLE STUDIES,
CALL 1-800-366-7788 (USA)
or 1-416-499-4615 (CANADA)

CONTENTS

AUTHOR

When Judy Hamlin was seventeen years old, she felt a call to Christian ministry during a church revival. That call remained on her mind as she grew up, married, reared a family, completed B.A., MLS, and Ph.D. degrees, and held a number of corporate and university positions.

Then, in 1985, after serving in several lay-leadership and consulting positions in her home church, Prestonwood Baptist in Dallas, she was asked by the pastor to become that church's first full-time minister to women and to coordinate its first small-group Bible study program. After much prayer, Judy heeded God's call.

This small-group course is a culmination of her experience in building the Prestonwood program and consulting with many other churches across the country in different phases of small-group ministry.

Judy lives in Austin with her husband, Newt, and son, Andrew. She is president of Small Group Services, consulting in small-group and women's ministries.

FOREWORD

In a time and culture when building positive relationships in families and churches often seems more and more difficult, it is exciting to see the ways in which Christian small groups are being rediscovered by churches as an important resource for Christian growth and ministry throughout the world. Small groups have always been important in the Church from the days of the New Testament to today. In places like Ethiopia and Kenya, China and Singapore, Brazil and Korea, as well as throughout the United States, the number of Christian small groups is exploding. People are discovering Christian community in new ways that help them to experience, expand, and apply their faith in many diverse and challenging settings.

One element of contemporary American society has been labeled "high tech, high touch." This slogan captures the increasing experience of so many people who find themselves involved day by day in a depersonalized, indifferent, and technological world, yet who are hungry for deep and meaningful personal relationships with people who know and care about them. Providing a place where love can be taught and experienced has always been a ministry of the followers of Jesus Christ, who commanded His disciples to "love one another."

Healthy small groups are one way in which churches can provide a context for love, nurture, and communication that moves beyond the polite and superficial to genuine love and ministry. There is good reason to believe that small groups are one of the most important resources to help both Christians and Christian churches grow in quality and in quantity. Renewal in denominations has almost always been marked by growing numbers of small-group fellowships. Many thousands of people throughout the world can give testimony to the importance of a Christian small group in their lives.

Judy Hamlin has provided a valuable resource to help group leaders and members understand the specific principles and skills that facilitate the beginning and growth of healthy small groups. Her practical, careful instructions are designed to reduce anxiety and increase effectiveness in carrying out this wonderful opportunity to interact with other people in discussions and activities that can make a genuine difference in their lives. To begin a new small group is to start on a new adventure in Christian community. Enjoy the journey!

Roberta Hestenes
President of Eastern College

ACKNOWLEDGMENTS

I greatly appreciate the many people who have contributed to the creation of this training material. Karen Hurston, a close friend and internationally known consultant on small groups, has unselfishly taught me about small groups. The members of the Dallas/Fort Worth Small-Group Association in Dallas, Texas, have been my support group and encouragers. In addition, I owe my deepest love and appreciation to my husband, Newt Hamlin, my toughest critic and an excellent editor.

Finally, I am especially grateful for the contributions of Darrell Skipworth and Diane Rolen for the outstanding art and forms included on these pages, and for Shirley Wilkins, a friend and typist who doesn't know the words "I can't."

BACKGROUND FOR THE TRAINER

God's plan for us to reach the world for Christ is clearly stated in Matthew 28:19-20 (NIV):

"Therefore go and make disciples of all nations, baptizing them in the name of the Father and of the Son and of the Holy Spirit, and teaching them to obey everything I have commanded you. And surely I am with you always, to the very end of the age."

Nowhere in Scripture does it tell us to "wait" for the unsaved world to come to us. We are told to "go." Romans 10:17 (NIV) reads, "Consequently, faith comes from hearing the message, and the message is heard through the word of Christ."

We must be prepared to teach the Word, as told in 2 Timothy 2:15 (NIV): "Do your best to present yourself to God as one approved, a workman who does not need to be ashamed and who correctly handles the word of truth."

We must reach out in our spheres of influence, as the Apostle Paul did in his: "I did not shrink from declaring to you anything that was profitable, and teaching you publicly and from house to house" (Acts 20:20).

It is the purpose of this training to present the "process," or "how-tos," of small-group dynamics. It is beyond the scope of this book to present "content" training, or the "how-tos" of presenting actual curriculum. The components of "process" training include the following: defining leadership characteristics, qualities, and styles; examining communications; describing effective witnessing and evangelism; developing relationships; and discussing promotion.

The genesis of this work comes from the great need many churches have expressed for training small-group leaders. Asked to list their primary problem, small-group coordinators have most frequently cited the need for leadership training materials. This training manual reflects my research into the best work done in the field of small groups, as well as my personal experience in coordinating a small-group program, enlisting leaders, developing training manuals and training, establishing church reporting systems, drafting many proposals for church groups, and helping other churches develop small-group ministries.

MANUAL FORMAT

This training manual is to be used with its sister publication, *The Small-Group Leaders Training Course Participant's Manual*. The training manual is designed in two-page spreads, with the student material (including answers) on the right side, and corresponding trainer's notes on the left. Valuable overflow information on certain topics is included in the appendix. It is vital for trainers to thoroughly prepare by studying the material, notes, and Scripture prior to each training session. Try not to omit any of the information.

The format of each trainer's page is as follows:

- Objective—the intended results for the students.
- Time—primarily for small-group exercises (lecture times vary).
- Process—the method of presenting the student material.

The process often includes exercises done within small sub-groups, which reinforce the main goals of the training. I strongly recommend following all of the guidelines, and doing all the exercises. During the evaluation of my training sessions, I have repeatedly been given two suggestions:

1. Have more interactive exercises.
2. Provide more time for them.

PERSONAL PREPARATION FOR TRAINING

You, the trainer, are the key to the success of this training. However, it should be comforting to know that you can successfully train without experience, provided you study this manual, read the recommended books, and spend time in prayer. (Read the job description for small-group coordinators, found on pages 189-190.)

You will find that your greatest assets, other than prayer, are your students. Adults bring experiences that will help them understand the materials. As you interact with them, be alert for valuable information and ideas to add to your notes.

The training manual also provides valuable information to help you develop your own leadership handbook (see page 157). You should compile your handbook prior to the training, and either review it with the group during training, or one-on-one with them prior to training.

There is much work to do, but the rewards are great. This training is designed to provide fun and fellowship and to help you build relationships, as well as to develop small-group leadership skills in yourself and others.

HOW TO LEAD THE SMALL-GROUP LEADER'S TRAINING COURSE

1. Have fun. Make the training enjoyable.

2. Provide experience. Help the participants "see" and "experience" everything you want them to retain.

3. Use rewards. Remember to reward with incentives. These gifts—for example, books, bookmarkers, highlighter pens, and potatoes, which can be used in a fun exercise—are to reward people for participating. Reward those who write on the flip chart. If you have a problem getting people to reconvene, try this: Before you break, tell them the first group back in place wins a prize (a good group prize is a bag of candy). And don't forget to applaud when appropriate.

4. Remember the time. Stay on schedule.

5. Set an example. Always model behavior you expect of your small group; explain everything thoroughly, then ask for questions.

6. Be yourself. Be real and don't be an "expert."

7. Affirm others. Always affirm your students when they contribute to the class.

8. Let the Spirit lead. Be open to the leading of the Holy Spirit. You may feel led to interject a song here and there, especially during a break or lunch; be flexible.

9. Help people get acquainted. If the training will be done in five two-hour sessions, tell the participants to sit with some people they do not know at each session. If you are going to follow the Friday evening/Saturday format, think of ways to reorganize the sub-groups from time to time, so new relationships can develop. Three possibilities are:

   a. Number the people 1, 2, 3, 4, and so on. Then group them by number.

   b. At the beginning of training, give a flip chart marker to each participant (have five each of a variety of colors). At the appropriate time, reorganize the groups by asking all those with a certain color to sit together.

   c. Try grouping by birthday month. (You may have to do a little adjusting of group sizes.)

10. Enlist volunteers. There are many ways to enlist volunteers. I had a lot of fun with the following

method: Have someone from each group volunteer to be a leader. Thank all of them, then explain that the people to their left are now the leaders. (Tell the group, "You can trust me when you volunteer.")

11. Allow freedom. When the sub-groups are working, don't listen in on their conversations. Let the group time be group time. You should, however, stay on schedule.

12. Allow for differences. Realizing that every training experience is different, be flexible and adaptable. I have never taught this course the same way twice. It will vary according to the members of the class—their levels of understanding, their personalities, and the experiences and stories they add to the training.

13. Use personal experience. Your personal experiences and anecdotes can make the training come alive. Use them whenever appropriate.

14. Sing. Use singing to begin sessions, especially if you consistently have a few latecomers. This allows a little time before you begin with content.

PRE-TRAINING DETAILS

1. Enlist potential leaders and hosts. This can be done in many ways: one-on-one, through your church newsletter or Sunday bulletin (see page 191), verbal announcements, and so on.

2. Develop a leadership questionnaire. Have each potential leader or host complete one (see pages 192-195), and then keep them on file.

3. Communicate. Write each participant to confirm training dates, times, room numbers, and so on. Express your excitement about the training and the ministry he or she has chosen.

4. Compile your handbook. Turn to page 158 and choose the pages that you need to include in your leadership handbook.

5. Make physical arrangements. Schedule the meeting room, arrange lunch and break snacks, and prepare additional handouts, such as song sheets.

6. Arrange for equipment. The necessary equipment includes flip charts, markers, and perhaps a sound system for a larger group, to use for speaking and for playing background Christian music as the group gathers.

7. Purchase incentive gifts. You will use incentives throughout the training, and they should relate to Bible study. Examples: prayer diaries; memory verse cards; small-group books, including *Using the Bible in Small Groups, How to Lead Small Groups,* and *My Utmost for His Highest*; highlighter pens; book markers; candy (for group gifts); white potatoes and straws (for a funny exercise).

8. Be prepared for each person. Have a name tag, a church leadership handbook, and a participant's manual for each group member.

9. Develop a song sheet. Use short choruses such as "Thank You, Lord," "Surely the Presence," "The Joy of the Lord," "This Is the Day," and "The Trees of the Field." You will use this song sheet at various times during the training.

10. Learn the "potato exercise." Practice the potato exercise described on page 120. You will want to let the participants try it before you show them how it's done.

11. Read the following books:

   ♦ Hestenes, Roberta. *Using the Bible in Groups*. Philadelphia: The Westminister Press, 1985.
   ♦ McBride, Neal F. *How to Lead Small Groups*. Colorado Springs: NavPress, 1990.

After reading the books, you may want to make additional notes in your training manual.

12. Be ready to evaluate. Develop an evaluation form to be used at the end of the course. The results will help you improve the training. (See the sample on page 198.)

SCHEDULE

The training material is divided into six sections. It can be taught using one of two formats. The ideal format is Friday evening from 6:30 to 9:30 p.m. and Saturday from 8:30 a.m. to 3:00 p.m. People with limited discretionary time can more easily commit to those hours. A sample agenda for Friday and Saturday follows:

FRIDAY
Fellowship and refreshments	6:30–7:00
Welcome	7:00–7:10
Introduction	7:10–7:30
Section 1 — Leadership	7:30–8:45
Characteristics	
Qualities	
Obstacles	
Questionnaire	
(Short break)	
Styles	
Questionnaire results	
Conversational prayer	
Small-group exercise	8:45–9:10
Review of church leadership handbook	9:10–9:30

SATURDAY
Continental breakfast	8:30–9:00
Section 2 — Communications — relationship building	9:00–10:00
Five levels	
Examples	
Skills	
Crossword puzzle	
Exercise	
Nonverbal skills	
Observations	
Questions	
Asking	
Answering	
Sharing	
Notes	
Small-group exercise	10:05–10:30
Break	10:30–10:45
Section 3 — Witnessing	10:45–11:45
Everyone should be prepared. Are you?	
Essentials of witnessing	
Effective communication	

Evangelism: then and now
Employing relationships
Effective friendship evangelism
Extended family member profile
Eight levels of spiritual development
Small-group exercise   11:45–12:10
"Eyes for My Community"   12:10–12:20

LUNCH   12:20–1:00

Section 4—Relationships   1:00–2:00
Covenant
Components
Chokers
Common problems
Clever "bees"
Calls and cards
Conducting a group
Commissioning others
Composition
Prayer
(Short break)
Circumstance case study   2:05–2:25
Section 5—Promotion and Review   2:25–3:00
Closing

An optional format is to offer the training in two-hour sessions on five consecutive Sunday evenings.

Week 1   Introduction, Leadership
Week 2   Review of church leadership handbook
          Communications, Questions
Week 3   Witnessing
Week 4   Relationships
Week 5   Circumstance Case Study, Promotion and Review

FACILITIES
The following room arrangement for training is highly recommended. This arrangement works with as few as fourteen people, and as many as forty. The following checklist should be used in preparing the facility:

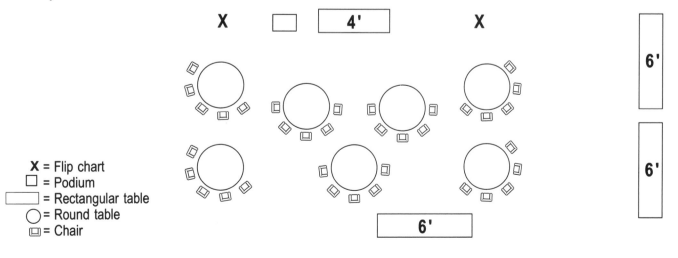

X = Flip chart
□ = Podium
▭ = Rectangular table
○ = Round table
▱ = Chair

15

Round tables, rather than square or rectangular, are preferable, to facilitate small-group exercises. This setup is not always possible. However, always accommodate sub-groups of four or five.

___ Round tables provided for participants

___ Chairs placed around each table so that everyone can face the leader (note the open space at each table). If possible, put only five chairs at each table.

___ Adequate lighting

___ Two flip charts at the front of the room

___ A variety of colored markers

___ A table at the front of the room for displaying materials the leader will use to supplement training

___ Rectangular tables located strategically in the room for sign-in, name tags, manuals, and refreshments

OPENING EACH TRAINING SESSION
Trainer's Opening Remarks
Give your background, and your vision for small groups. Explain why you are personally excited about having groups in your church.

Open in prayer.

Welcome!
Thank the participants for their time, and acknowledge that they could have made other choices.

Sing one or two songs from the song sheet.

Materials
Review all the materials as you distribute them.

Instructions
Encourage everyone to bring his or her Bible to class. Have extra Bibles to distribute to those who did not bring their own.

Remind the group that you will begin and end on time. *And do!*

Ask for a volunteer who will serve as time-keeper. This person will participate in all activities, but will have the added responsibility of keeping track of time, and ringing a bell when time is up for all small-group work. At the end of training, reward the timekeeper.

AFTER THE TRAINING COURSE
1. Pray. Set aside regular time to pray for your small-group ministry and its leadership.

2. Communicate. Regularly contact group leaders. Show concern and help them solve problems.

3. Plan ongoing training. Provide regular leadership training sessions. (See sample agenda, page 198.)

4. Enlist new leadership. One-on-one enlistment is the most effective method. Preparing co-leaders to assume leadership is effective, but they should understand the possible position upgrade when they are enlisted. Current leaders can identify potential leaders. Finally, a "church leadership list" can identify potential group leaders, since people are generally ready to change areas of service every two years. Maintain contact with people who have expressed an interest in small-group

ministry; inform them of training dates and ministry needs (i.e., we currently need five host homes). If you mail a newsletter to current leadership, always include potential leaders in your mailing. (See page 199 for a sample potential leadership list.)

5. Promote small groups. Use church newsletters, bulletins, and brochures to update and promote small-group ministry, announce training opportunities, and share testimonies. Encourage the pastor to preach a sermon series on groups and to make announcements during services. During Sunday services, enlist group leaders to distribute ministry brochures, assign people to groups, and answer questions. This can be done at a ministry table or booth in the church atrium.

6. Prepare for growth. Encourage co-leaders to attend training and prepare to start new groups. Offer initial leadership training quarterly. Keep a waiting list of trainees—you need at least fourteen for good small-group dynamics.

7. Form a committee. Create a steering committee within your church structure to oversee the small-group ministry. The steering committee will give direction to the ministry, provide representation in the church governing body, and help build awareness and acceptance of groups.

8. Make use of the library. Provide your church library with a list of books on small groups, which should be made available for leadership training. (See pages 205-206.)

9. Spend time together. Plan a yearly retreat for leaders and hosts. Also, have at least one annual social activity for them.

10. Placement. Promote placement of church members in groups. Develop flyers or brochures listing available groups. Assign people by using a three-part form (name, address, telephone, leader, host, time, day of meeting), giving one part to the visitor, one to a group leader, and one to the group coordinator. The form is a helpful way to keep people from dropping through the cracks and allows the group leader to personally invite visitors. This allows the coordinator to place people in groups based on interests, age, and so on, and helps groups grow by sending visitors to those that are new or small.

11. Reporting system. Establish a system for reporting attendance records to the church to be published with other statistics. (See pages 177-180.)

INTRODUCTION

THE VALUE OF SMALL GROUPS

OBJECTIVE: Instill in the participants a call and commitment to the small-group ministry.

TIME: Three minutes (sub-group time).

PROCESS:

1. Select a leader in each group.

2. Instruct each leader to read the "call" and "commission" aloud, as the group members read silently.

3. As a large group, discuss the "call" and "commission." Ask, "What excites you about this call and commission?" "What, if anything, makes you nervous about leading a small group?"

THE VALUE OF SMALL GROUPS

CALL

Small groups are very valuable. They give Christians opportunities to invite neighbors, coworkers, friends, or relatives to a place other than church, and to introduce them to Jesus Christ.

No one is more vital to the success of a small group than its leader. This leadership training will help you develop communication skills and identify your leadership styles for maximum effectiveness. Also, the dynamics of leadership that you learn will carry over in business meetings, PTA meetings, family discussions, and more.

You will receive two other important benefits from small-group training: improved prayer life and evangelism training to equip you to reach your family, friends, and coworkers.

COMMISSION

The [instructions] which you have heard from me, along with many witnesses, transmit and entrust (as a deposit) to reliable and faithful men who will be competent and qualified to teach others also. (2 Timothy 2:2, AMP)

THE BIBLICAL BASIS FOR SMALL GROUPS

OBJECTIVE: Review the biblical basis for small groups.

TIME: Will vary.

PROCESS:

1. Ask group members to read each verse or passage.

2. After each one is read, discuss key words such as the following:

    Continually
    Devoting
    Teaching
    Fellowship
    Prayer
    Continuing
    Praising God
    Every day
    Preaching
    Declaring
    House to house

THE BIBLICAL BASIS FOR SMALL GROUPS

And they were continually devoting themselves to the apostles' teaching and to fellowship, to the breaking of bread and to prayer. (Acts 2:42)

And day by day continuing with one mind in the temple, and breaking bread from house to house, they were taking their meals together with gladness and sincerity of heart, praising God, and having favor with all the people. And the Lord was adding to their number day by day those who were being saved. (Acts 2:46-47)

And every day, in the temple and from house to house, they kept right on teaching and preaching Jesus as the Christ. (Acts 5:42)

How I did not shrink from declaring to you anything that was profitable, and teaching you publicly and from house to house. (Acts 20:20)

7

GETTING TO KNOW YOU

OBJECTIVES: Get to know each other.
Have fun.
Recognize that we should not prejudge people.

TIME: Eight minutes.

PROCESS:

1. On a flip chart, write three statements — two true, one false — about yourself.

   ◆ I love to cook.

   ◆ I am 5'2" tall.

   ◆ I have a puppy that is not housebroken.

2. Tell the group that one statement is false. For each statement, ask how many think it is false. Record the number.

3. Then reveal the false statement, pointing out how many judged you incorrectly.

4. Appoint a leader for each sub-group and repeat this activity.

5. When the groups are done, ask the participants if they were surprised at the number they judged incorrectly. Then explain that we all tend to prejudge people, based on first impressions. In small groups, it is vital that we accept people unconditionally.

GETTING TO KNOW YOU

1. Write three personal statements—two true and one false.

2. Read each statement and ask how many think it is false. Write down that number.

3. Reveal the false statement.

_____

_____

_____

_____

_____

_____

_____

_____

_____

_____

_____

_____

_____

_____

WHERE ARE YOU?

OBJECTIVE: Identify areas for personal improvement.

TIME: Three minutes (individual time).

PROCESS:

1. Have each person do the exercise on page 27.

2. Ask for two volunteers to go to the two flip charts. Label one "Strengths," and the other "Areas to Improve." Have people call out traits, listing five or six on each chart.

3. Point out that the purpose of this training is to improve weak areas, as well as reinforce strong areas.

WHERE ARE YOU?

DIRECTIONS: On a scale of 20 to 100, 100 being the most positive, rate yourself on the following traits by placing an "x" beneath the number that is applicable. Then record your three greatest strengths and three areas needing improvement.

	20	40	60	80	100
Enthusiastic					
Nice (friendly)					
Ready (prepared)					
Adaptable (flexible)					
Positive attitude					
Withholds judgment					
Sensitive					
Wise					
Communication skills					
Good eye contact					
Smiles					
Listens					
Remembers names					
Empathy (understanding)					
Genuinely helpful					
Good appearance					
Courteous					
Solves problems					
Organized					
Personal Bible study					
Prayer					
Intercessory prayer					
Belief (faith)					
Obedient					
Caring					
Dedicated					

STRENGTHS

AREAS TO IMPROVE

9

1

LEADERSHIP

FIVE CHARACTERISTICS
OF EFFECTIVE BIBLE DISCUSSION LEADERS

OBJECTIVE: Identify characteristics of an effective Bible discussion leader.

TIME: Will vary depending on your research and lecture.

PROCESS:

1. Simply fill in the blanks, adding your comments or personal experiences; then have group members read the Scripture as time permits.

   Question 1: a. An effective leader has a right relationship to God's call and purpose in his or her life.

   b. An effective leader gives out of the overflow of God's Word in his or her life.

   c. If a person is unable to follow, there is a question about his or her leadership abilities. Obedience is necessary in order to be able to lead.

   Question 2: People are looking for others who will pray for them.

   Question 3: In his seminar entitled "People Sharing Jesus: Witness and Soul-Winning," Darrell Robinson tells us that "your attitude will make the difference in your witness. True enthusiasm is a faith attitude. *Enthuse* is derived from a compound Greek word . . . literally translated—'in God.' When you are in God and God is in you, you are enthused."

   Question 4: We live in a cold, cynical world. People do not often experience compassion, and they need to see it modeled in you.

   Question 5: Good leadership is created through study and preparation. Fill in the blanks in the box, and complete the principle point of the study.

2. Optional discussion: Ask if someone would share a story about a person who displayed these characteristics and what effect it had on that person.

FIVE CHARACTERISTICS
OF EFFECTIVE BIBLE DISCUSSION LEADERS

1. The characteristic of _obedience_

   An effective leader is in right relationship to

   a. _God_

   b. _God's Word_

   c. _God's people and persons in positions of authority_

2. The characteristic of _prayer_

   Prayer is vital in our relationship with God (see 2 Chronicles 7:14, Philippians 4:6-7).

3. The characteristic of _belief_

   Without faith, it is impossible to please God and be of direct benefit to others (see Luke 22:32, 1 Corinthians 16:13-14).

4. The characteristic of _compassion_ combined with _clear communication_. Scripture directs us to speak

   the truth in love (see Ephesians 4:15), and to be a vessel of love to others.

5. The characteristic of _study and preparation_

   Leaders must be teachable in order to correctly handle the word of truth (see 2 Timothy 2:15).

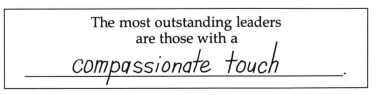

The most outstanding leaders
are those with a

compassionate touch.

12

FOUR WINNING QUALITIES OF LEADERSHIP

OBJECTIVE: Identify winning leadership qualities.

TIME: Will vary depending on the examples you give.

PROCESS:

Open by reading 1 Thessalonians 2:1-12.

1. Have someone read each verse. Then ask the group what word belongs in the blank. Discuss the sentence that follows. Give a personal example of determined leadership if possible. Whether there is a high or low turnout, focus on those people who are present. God has a purpose for those gathered. Be determined.

2. Have someone read verse 3 and discuss the statement.

3. After verse 7 is read, you might note the great example of the gentle style of a mother with her child. Ask for other examples.

4. Read verses 11 and 12. In the secular world, we are viewed by what we do: at the grocery store, we make choices and spend money; at work, we must develop or produce products; at home, we are mommies and daddies.

Fill in the blanks in the box. Challenge each person to strive for Paul's leadership qualities.

FOUR WINNING QUALITIES OF LEADERSHIP

Paul showed four qualities of leadership while at Thessalonica. Read 1 Thessalonians 2:1-12.

1. Verse 2 _Determination_

At times we get discouraged, but if we are God-called, we can carry on with determination.

2. Verse 3 _Pure motives_

We should not lead to outdo others, but like Paul, we should have pure motives.

3. Verse 7 _Gentle style_

People in the world today are exposed to harshness and cynicism.

4. Verses 11-12 _Personal focus_

People need a place to be accepted for who they are, not for what they can do. This is a refreshing change.

Paul was effective because he was

determined , had

pure motives , a

gentle style , and a

personal focus on people

under his care.

13

OBSTACLES TO EFFECTIVE LEADERSHIP

OBJECTIVE: Identify causes of failure as a group leader.

TIME: Three minutes (sub-group time).

PROCESS:

1. Complete each question, adding the additional ideas that follow.

   Question 1: Wrong motives for leadership. Wrong motives can block a leader's spiritual growth, and hamper a group's spiritual progress. Wrong motives include seeking power, authority, or position; seeking to fill an emotional need, such as acceptance or approval; or seeking acclaim. Right motives include glorifying God, obeying His call, loving the Lord and Christian brethren, and advancing the Kingdom of God.

   Question 2: A sense of inadequacy. Leaders can be plagued with doubts and insecurities. However, they must avoid demanding more of themselves than the Lord does, or becoming enslaved to others' expectations rather than the Lord's. Remember, God often uses the weak to "confound the strong" (1 Corinthians 1:27, 2 Corinthians 12:9-10).

   Question 3: Fear of failure. Every leader should expect to make mistakes; it's part of the learning process.

   Question 4: Discouragement and disappointment. Things do not always turn out as we like. The important point is to focus on Christ. Remember 1 Thessalonians 2:2, and be determined.

   Question 5: Appearing spiritually dry. Spiritual dryness is usually caused by an absence of prayer, Bible study, holy living, and concentration of purpose. One danger of leadership is being so busy that we neglect our own relationship with the Lord. We must continue praying and studying, and give out of our overflow.

   Question 6: Unrealistic schedules. Leaders must base both personal and group schedules on God-directed priorities. It may be necessary to cut back on activities not planned by the Lord. Rest is part of His plan, and our bodies are the temple of His Spirit. Good time management is a leadership responsibility.

   Question 7: Improper handling of relational conflicts. Personality clashes, jealousy, competitiveness, and so on, must be dealt with through prayer and honest love.

   Question 8: Conflicts with authority. Problems arise when a leader disobeys God-anointed authority. Leaders are to respect and submit to authority.

   Question 9: Undue focus on attendance. The leader must focus on those present, not on those absent, and minister to current needs.

2. Tell the sub-groups to list three additional obstacles to effective leadership. Have a volunteer write them on a flip chart. Possible responses could include:

Several canceled meetings

Changing the day and time for meeting

Being unapproachable

Lack of leadership skills

Feelings of superiority

Fear of success

Not being flexible

Disagreement of purpose among participants

LEADERSHIP

OBSTACLES TO EFFECTIVE LEADERSHIP

Factors that can cause people to leave a group, possibly causing the group to die:

1. _Wrong motives_ for leadership

2. A sense of _inadequacy_

3. Fear of _failure_

4. _Discouragement_ and _disappointment_

5. Appearing _spiritually dry_

6. Unrealistic _schedules_

7. Improper handling of _relational conflicts_

8. Conflicts with _authority_

9. Undue focus on _attendance_

14

LEADERSHIP QUESTIONNAIRE

OBJECTIVE: Help each participant begin to identify his or her personal leadership style.

TIME: Allow five minutes to complete the leadership questionnaire.

PROCESS:

1. Have each participant respond to the leadership questionnaire.

2. Explain that a leader's style has a direct influence on a group, and can either motivate or hinder its development.

LEADERSHIP QUESTIONNAIRE

The following are difficult situations that might face a small-group leader. How would you handle each one? Circle the letter of your response.

1. One group member is using half the time in each meeting to tell about her many personal and work problems. Other group members are clearly unhappy.
    a. Tell her firmly in the meeting that she does not have the right to monopolize group time.
    b. Tell the other group members that it's all right; they'll get to the study in a bit.
    c. Call her aside after the meeting. Explain the problem, the effect she is having on the group, and your interest in helping. Then, suggest getting together before future meetings, when necessary. Pray with her.
    d. Refer her to a counselor.

2. You developed a well-researched Bible study on a topic you feel is very important. The night of the study, one of your members is very upset because of a personal problem.
    a. Teach your Bible study without reference to the situation.
    b. Visit with him and the group about his personal problem and save your planned Bible study for a later date.
    c. Lead a period of prayer and ministry, followed by a shortened presentation of your planned Bible study.
    d. Suggest a source of professional help for him. Then explain the importance of the Bible study topic for the evening.

3. One member of your group keeps insisting that you are spending too much time in prayer and not enough time in Bible study.
    a. Tell him if he doesn't like the group, he can go elsewhere.
    b. Tell him to relax; the group will get to the Bible study eventually.
    c. Discuss his comment with the group and ask how the others feel about it.
    d. Say to him, "You may be correct, but this is the decision I have made." Then, help him find a class or group that concentrates on strong biblical teaching.

4. Attendance in your group is lagging, and those who do come are straggling in late.
    a. Firmly tell everyone that they should come on time.
    b. Tell them that only one or two were on time, but next week, maybe three will be.
    c. After group input, change the location, the day of the week, or the time of day.
    d. Call the members, remind them of the agreed-upon time, and start the next meeting on time regardless of who is present.

STYLES OF LEADERSHIP

OBJECTIVE: Understand four leadership styles.

TIME: Five minutes (sub-group time); one minute presentation time per group.

PROCESS:

1. Assign one leadership style to each sub-group. If you have more than four groups in training, each style will be assigned to more than one group.

2. Instruct the sub-groups to review the characteristics of their style, then give them five minutes to prepare a presentation of that style for the larger group. They may use any method (role play or lecture) or class aid (flip chart or blackboard).

3. Following each one-minute presentation, ask the large group which style was depicted.

4. This exercise can be a lot of fun. If you have an outstanding presentation, reward that group with a prize, such as a bag of candy.

5. After the presentations, fill in the words below the wheel, the web, the net, and the cogwheels on pages 40-43.

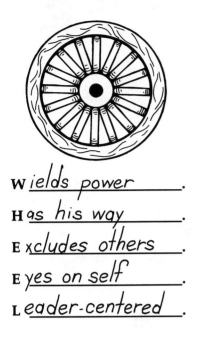

W _ields power_ .
H _as his way_ .
E _xcludes others_ .
E _yes on self_ .
L _eader-centered_ .

STYLES OF LEADERSHIP—AUTOCRATIC

CHARACTERISTICS

◆ Maintains total control, treating group members as listeners and followers.

◆ Determines goals and policies.

◆ Is more interested in subject matter (content) than people (process).

◆ Makes all decisions, disregarding others' views.

◆ Talks too much.

◆ Focuses attention on self.

◆ Regards group members as puppets.

IN BIBLE STUDY

◆ Asks and answers all questions.

> This is not an appropriate leadership style for a small-group Bible study.

STYLES OF LEADERSHIP—AUTHORITATIVE

CHARACTERISTICS

◆ Maintains strong control, yet actively involves members in the discussions.

◆ Has a definite purpose and plan, but is open to modification.

◆ Is active and energetic, and seeks the involvement of others.

◆ Is prepared to give necessary direction and support.

◆ Uses communication skills to involve others.

◆ Takes responsibility until others can assume it.

◆ Uses personal power to empower others.

IN BIBLE STUDY

◆ Prepares and asks questions, then elicits members' responses.

W _orkaholic_____.
E _mpowers others_.
B _lends the group_.

This style of leadership is helpful in the beginning stages of a group's life. As the group matures, flexibility and sensitivity become imperative.

17

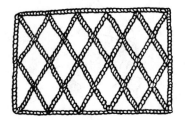

N *oncontrolling*.

E *quips others*.

T *enderhearted*.

STYLES OF LEADERSHIP—DEMOCRATIC

CHARACTERISTICS

◆ Shares control with members.

◆ Shares leadership responsibility.

◆ Believes in other people.

◆ Creates a sense of security and belonging.

◆ Ensures that others have leadership opportunities.

◆ Makes certain that if he withdraws, the group will not fall apart.

◆ Sees that the group discusses all policies.

IN A BIBLE STUDY

◆ Involves others in leading the Bible study.

> This is the most appropriate leadership style for a small-group Bible study.

STYLES OF LEADERSHIP—LAISSEZ-FAIRE

CHARACTERISTICS

◆ Exercises minimal control, allowing members to direct.

◆ Doesn't prepare; lets discussion drift.

◆ Doesn't seem to care.

◆ Causes the group to accomplish very little.

◆ Encourages fragmentation through lack of discipline.

◆ Makes no attempt to regulate events.

◆ Lacks courage in making plans.

IN A BIBLE STUDY

◆ Asks general questions, then is silent.

> This type of leadership is highly discouraged. The vacuum allows a domineering member to take charge.

C _onceding_ .
O _missive_ .
G _loomy_ .

19

QUESTIONNAIRE RESULTS

OBJECTIVE: Have each participant identify his or her personal leadership style.

TIME: Will vary.

PROCESS:

1. After the participants complete question 1, ask how many had the most As, Bs, Cs, and Ds.

2. Reveal the styles for A, B, C, and D, filling in the blank below each letter.

3. Then have each person do question 2.

4. Close with the lecture note below.
   As a rule, authoritative and democratic styles are most appropriate for a small-group Bible study. An authoritative leader is best when the group is beginning. As the weeks go on, other members should be drawn into leadership by asking them to perform certain functions, such as leading the opening prayer, keeping a journal of prayer requests and answers, or researching a difficult Bible passage encountered during the study. Perhaps someone will use the "gift of baking" and provide a cake for refreshments. The leader should gradually do less leading, and encourage more and more participation. As a result, the group will become a cohesive, democratic unit.

QUESTIONNAIRE RESULTS

1. Turn to page 15. How many times did you choose each letter?

    A _____

    B _____

    C _____

    D _____

2. Circle the letter that identified you *most often*.

A

Autocratic

B

Laissez-Faire

C

Democratic

D

Authoritative

CONVERSATIONAL PRAYER

OBJECTIVE: Learn how to conduct a conversational prayer time.

TIME: Will vary.

PROCESS: Lecture

CONVERSATIONAL PRAYER

1. Limit the time for prayer requests. Often more time is spent making requests than praying. One solution is to skip the requests, and simply begin praying for specific needs.

2. Use conversational tones in audible prayer. Use everyday language. A group meeting is not the place for religious speeches in prayer. The leader's modeling of conversational prayer is pivotal.

3. Cultivate a consciousness of God's presence. All prayers should be directed to Him. Never pray to the group. Kneeling or holding hands can enhance an attitude of prayer.

4. Be brief. God does not hear us on the basis "of . . . many words" (Matthew 6:7), but rather on the basis of faith (Matthew 17:20, Hebrews 11:6). Jesus modeled brief prayer throughout His ministry (Matthew 26:39,42; Mark 15:34; Luke 23:34,46; John 11;41-43). Each person should pray in one or two sentences, then allow others to pray. Pray so an eight-year-old child could understand.

5. Have one person pray about one topic. In conversations, only one topic at a time should be shared by the group. Only one person at a time should pray. One person's prayer might focus on a topic such as prayer for wisdom in a job situation. Another person might then pray for wisdom in a family situation.

6. Agree in prayer. When one group member is praying, the others should silently agree; there is much power in prayer of agreement (Matthew 18:19-20). During the prayer, others can verbalize agreement by short responses such as "yes, Lord"; "hear this prayer"; and "answer that prayer, Lord."

7. Be spontaneous. Informality, honesty, and love are all vital. Stay away from ritualistic, memorized prayers—we are in relationship with a living God "who has been tempted in all things as we are" (Hebrews 4:15).

8. Allow for silence. Silence is not an uncomfortable space to be filled with unnecessary words. A waiting silence to hear the voice of God can be the most reverent portion of a group's prayer time.

9. Pray with and for each other. It is appropriate to follow someone's prayer with a request related to an expressed need or concern. Example: After John prays for his wife in the hospital, Ann might add, "God, please strengthen John and the children during this difficult period." Peter could then say, "Lord, we ask that You provide for the financial needs of John's family during his wife's hospitalization."

10. Pray for each member of the group. Each one might ask for a prayer request from the person on his right, and then pray for that request as the prayer moves around the circle.

11. Expect God to guide. As the group is praying, be prepared at any time to confess, to uphold, to rejoice, to accept, to exhort, to forgive, to agree, and to weep.

12. Be creative. At various times try the different types of prayer: adoration (praise), thanksgiving, confession, commitment, and intercession. Also, choose various topics to focus on, such as family relationships, needs of the local church, community problems, national government, and authorities.

Fill in the blanks in the box, which state the primary purposes of conversational prayer.

CONVERSATIONAL PRAYER

KEY PRINCIPLES

1. Limit the time for prayer _requests_.

2. Use _conversational tones_ in audible prayer.

3. Cultivate a consciousness of _God's presence_.

4. Be _brief_.

5. Have one _person_ pray about one _topic_.

6. _Agree_ in prayer.

7. Be _spontaneous_.

8. Allow for _silence_.

9. Pray _with_ and _for_ each other.

10. Pray for each member of the _group_.

11. Expect God to _guide_.

12. Be _creative_.

The primary purposes of conversational prayer in a group are:

1. To _provide_ an opportunity for people to pray together;

2. That each member may realize the presence of _Christ_ in the midst of the group.

SMALL-GROUP EXERCISE

OBJECTIVES: Establish a small group.
Lead a conversational prayer.
Learn the components of a small-group exercise.

TIME: Twenty to twenty-five minutes; give a five-minute warning before ending.

PROCESS:

1. Instruct the groups to appoint a leader and work through the small-group exercise.

2. As the instructor, you may be tempted to walk around and listen in on the groups. *Don't.*
   Let the groups remain private.

3. Following the small-group exercise, lead the large group in a review of components of the exercise.

SMALL-GROUP EXERCISE

OPENING

Introduce yourself.

PRAYER

Begin with short conversational prayers.

SHARING

Name a leadership quality of a person who has greatly influenced your life. Why do you value that quality?

REVIEW

a. Review the characteristics of effective leadership (page 12). Remembering a positive experience in a small group (Bible study, committee, or Sunday school class), identify a characteristic that the group leader possessed, and why you thought it was important.

b. Review the obstacles to effective leadership (page 14). Which one do you think is the most frequent, and how can it best be overcome?

c. Review the four styles of leadership (pages 16-19). Which one do you display?

CLOSE

Spend more time in conversational prayer.

2

COMMUNICATION AND QUESTIONS

BUILDING RELATIONSHIPS

OBJECTIVE: Identify three relationship-building periods of a small-group meeting.

TIME: Will vary.

PROCESS:

1. Before the meeting begins:
   You should have all preliminary details covered so you and the leadership team can greet members as they arrive.

2. During the meeting:
   Each person brings three social needs to the group:

   a. Need for belonging. To feel we belong, we need to feel connected to a family that holds Jesus Christ central.

   b. Need for significance. When the leader identifies a participant's gifts and gives him or her responsibilities, the participant will acquire a feeling of significance.

   c. Need for acceptance. Before participants attend a group, they wonder if the other members will accept them. To develop that acceptance, leaders should refrain from criticism, which will lead to lack of trust. Be positive and build each other up.

3. After the meeting:
   Leaders should be willing to visit with members who do not feel comfortable bringing up a sensitive need in the open group. This is a good time for building relationships. In addition, three other opportunities exist: (a) calling members, especially those with known needs; (b) establishing prayer partners; (c) arranging social activities.

Filling in the blanks in the box will provide insight into interpersonal communication.

BUILDING RELATIONSHIPS

There are three periods in a small group to build relationships.

1. _Before_ the meeting begins

2. _During_ the meeting

Each person brings three social needs:

  a. The need for _belonging_

  b. The need for _significance_

  c. The need for _acceptance_

3. _After_ the meeting

Good interpersonal communication requires:

1. A _positive_ view of people as God's creatures;

2. _Openness_ and honesty;

3. A commitment to be _persistent_ in relationships;

4. Courage and willingness to take _risks_ ;

5. The _development_ and use of certain communication skills.

24

COMMUNICATION—FIVE LEVELS

OBJECTIVE: Identify five levels of communication.

TIME: Will vary.

PROCESS: Lecture

1. Cliché conversation. Discussing "safe" public information takes place during the first few minutes of a meeting. Topics include the weather, family and friends, and current affairs.

2. Sharing information and facts. People talk generally about events, ideas, and facts, but not about themselves, their commitments, and their beliefs about Scripture.

3. Sharing ideas and opinions. This deeper level of communication involves a willingness to talk about personal ideas and opinions. There is some risk-taking at this level.

4. Sharing feelings. People are willing to risk telling group members what they *feel*, not just what they *think*. Members are less protective and more open.

5. Peak communication. The deepest level of communication involves openness, transparency, and self-disclosure. It is a risky and rare but powerful level of communication. Think of a close relationship you have; what you most remember is probably peak communication.

Fill in the blanks in the box.

COMMUNICATION—FIVE LEVELS

1. Cliché _Conversation_

2. Sharing _information_ and _facts_

3. Sharing _ideas_ and _opinions_

4. Sharing _feelings_

5. _Peak_ communication

Much of any _relationship_ is built through the proper use of _communication skills_. Communication is both _verbal_ and _nonverbal_, and involves conveying _feelings_, _ideas_, _opinions_, _information_, and _wishes_. A strong and cohesive small group will have deepening levels of communication among its members.

25

COMMUNICATION EXAMPLE

OBJECTIVE: Demonstrate levels of communication.

TIME: Two minutes to read the script.

PROCESS:

1. Have two volunteers assume the roles of Marilyn and Becky and read the conversation on page 57.

2. Explain that this example is drastic, but that it demonstrates that close relationships reach a deeper level of communication in a group setting.

3. On occasion, a group member may be in tears and express a deep need (peak communication). Put your arms around the person, have the group pray for him or her, then return to the study. After the meeting, spend more time together.

COMMUNICATION EXAMPLE

LEVEL 1

Marilyn: Hi, how was the weather in Florida?

Becky: Beautiful; 70 degrees most of the time.

Marilyn: You must have had a wonderful time.

LEVEL 2

Becky: Yes, but I was reading about the famine in Ethiopia and had
         to stop and think. Do you ever think of people being hungry?

LEVEL 3/LEVEL 4

Marilyn: Yes, hunger is a real sad thing for me. I've seen those chil-
         dren on television. It breaks my heart. I don't know why we
         don't do more.

LEVEL 5

Becky: You know, starvation is not just on television. My sister
         became anorectic and literally starved herself. She died a
         month ago.

COMMUNICATION SKILLS

OBJECTIVE: Identify twelve ways to use communication skills.

TIME: Will vary.

PROCESS: Lecture

1. Listening. Physically and emotionally focus on the person who is talking; convey your interest and intention to listen. Face the person to whom you are listening; lean forward if you're sitting, relax and maintain good eye contact. Use brief phrases like *yes, really?* and *how interesting!* to show the speaker you are attentive. Listening is a real art, and is just as important to effective communication as speaking.

2. Seeking information and opinions. Use questions with members who have not spoken recently, and those who have good ideas or opinions. The use of first names is important. Examples: "Mary, what do you think about the second question?" "Joe, I'd be interested in your opinion on this subject."

3. Clarifying. Misunderstanding can arise when we assume we understand a speaker's meaning. When the meaning is unclear, ask a question for clarification. Examples: "I'm not sure what you meant. Could you please restate that?" "Could you repeat that and say a little more about what you mean?" Clarification is complimentary, as it shows a speaker you are listening and attentive.

4. Paraphrasing. A listener restating a speaker's thought or idea in his own words demonstrates careful listening and concern. Examples: "This is what I heard you saying. . . . Is that it?" "Mark, your central concern is. . . ." "David, your reactions seem to be. . . ."

5. Justifying. This involves asking people to give reasons for what they have said, and should be done in a positive, non-argumentative way. Justifying helps a group stay on a subject. Examples: "Where do you find that in the passage we're studying?" "Why do you say that?" "What is the connection between what we were discussing and your comment?"

6. Re-directing. When a group member continues to address all his questions and comments to the leader rather than to the group, use re-directing. Using names, encourage members to talk with each other. If Mary continues to focus on the leader, the leader might respond to her question, "Tom what do you think about Mary's last question?" "How would you answer that Tom?" This is particularly effective in involving new members in the discussion.

7. Extending. This involves adding to or expanding a line of thought in a discussion. After an answer is given, or a comment made, the leader might ask, "Does any one have anything to add to what has been said?" or, "Is there anything else someone would like to comment on at this point?"

8. Summarizing. At various points in a group discussion, it is helpful to briefly summarize and highlight what has been previously said. This technique works effectively when a group gets bogged down, since it outlines where the discussion has been and should be going. The leader should summarize carefully, not omitting group members' names and ideas.

9. Affirming. It is always important to recognize and affirm the person who is talking. To one you might say, "Thank you for your comment." To another you might add, "That's an interesting point." Never tell a person he is wrong. Simply redirect the question to others: "What do the rest of you think?" Even when a comment seems unimportant, the speaker is important.

10. Being concrete and personal. Use "I" messages instead of "you" messages. Communication improves when members take responsibility for their own ideas and feelings, using the personal pronoun "I." To say "I feel" or "I think" is much more direct and helpful than "Some people think" or "Some believe."

11. Being personally implicated. When a discussion seems too general, vague or abstract, a "personal implication question" helps keep the conversation more direct and specific. Examples: "What is your opinion about that?" "How would what you are talking about affect you personally?" "Have you ever struggled with this issue yourself?" "Sometimes we are abstract when discussing Scripture; how does it affect you day to day?" "How does this scripture affect my daily life?"

12. Handling talkative and silent members. Excessively talkative members can be handled through the proper use of group dynamics, nonverbal communication, and the seating arrangement. Eye contact is important: the leader should break eye contact with the talkative person (sit beside him, not across from him), and maintain consistent eye contact with a silent member (sit opposite him). When the talkative member pauses in the middle of a lengthy speech, the leader should break in and say, "I'd like to hear from someone who has not spoken yet." The leader might direct a question to a silent member: "Jim, what do you think is meant in verse 2?" Problems can cause people to talk too much, so try to visit with this person after the study. Ask him to observe the next two Bible studies and determine who is contributing and who is not.

COMMUNICATION SKILLS

1. Listening

2. Seeking information and opinions

3. Clarifying

4. Paraphrasing

5. Justifying

6. Redirecting

7. Extending

8. Summarizing

9. Affirming

10. Being concrete and personal

11. Being personally implicated

12. Handling talkative and silent members

CROSSWORD PUZZLE

OBJECTIVE: Demonstrate knowledge of communication skills.

TIME: Five minutes.

PROCESS:

Have everyone complete the puzzle, and reward the first one finished. Be sure you check the answers out loud, both for a review and for accuracy.

CROSSWORD PUZZLE

ACROSS

2. To draw out a reluctant speaker

5. Using an "I" statement

7. Retelling in one's own words

9. Use when a person talks only to the leader

10. Use to make a statement clear

11. Giving reasons for what has been said

12. Use seating to overcome

DOWN

1. Give consistent eye contact

3. To positively recognize

4. To build an expanded line of thought

6. Pay attention to the speaker

8. Highlighting a previous discussion

28

COMMUNICATION EXERCISE

OBJECTIVE: Identify communication skills.

TIME: Ten minutes.

PROCESS:

1. Tell everyone to read through the case studies, then identify communication skills in each line individually.

2. Compare notes within sub-groups (ten minutes).

3. Reconvene as a large group, read each line, and call for responses to each.

COMMUNICATION EXERCISE

Members in the following small-group case study are:

Joe—the discussion leader
Sally—a shy group member
John—a retired businessman
Lois—a new Christian
Diane—a co-leader

INSTRUCTIONS:

1. Read the case study.

2. Make marginal notes on communication skills being used by each group member.

3. Compare your notes with others in your small group.

CASE STUDY: MATTHEW 6:24-34

Joe: What do you think was the main point Jesus was trying to make with His listeners in this passage?   *2*

Sally: Was He telling them never to worry because God would take care of them?   *3, 17*

Joe: That's correct, Sally. Yet Jesus is emphasizing even more. John, will you put verse 33 in your own words for us?

9, 5, 6, 2, 7, 10, 4

John: It seems to me Jesus is saying that if we seek to grow spiritually, all our physical needs will be provided.   *4, 10*

Lois: I'm not certain I understand what "grow spiritually means."
5, 3, 2, 10

Joe: That's a valid statement, Lois. Would someone like to explain what it means to "grow spiritually"?   *2, 9, 4, 7, 6*

Sally: Is it going to church and reading your Bible?   *2, 1, 3*

Joe: Yes, Sally, these are things that help us grow spiritually. Diane, how would you add to what Sally said?   *6, 7, 9, 10*

DIRECTOR

Diane: There is so much involved in growing spiritually, just like all that goes on when we grow physically. Like Sally said, it helps to go to church, read the Bible, and spend personal time in prayer and Bible study; it means learning how Jesus lived and becoming like Him in our own lives.   1, 8, 9

John: Could we say that it is a way of behavior and attitude of life?
                                  2, 3, 8

Joe: Good point, John. And of what would that attitude of life consist?   2, 9, 11

Lois: An attitude of wanting to please God in all that we do and think; is that it?   3

Joe: Excellent, Lois. When every action and thought is focused on pleasing God and bringing honor and glory to Him, He is going to meet our every need. What a reassurance and promise that is!
        Next week we will continue in our study of the Beatitudes.

        8, 9, 10

NONVERBAL COMMUNICATION SKILLS

OBJECTIVES: Recognize nonverbal communication skills.
Differentiate among effective and ineffective nonverbal skills.

TIME: Will vary.

PROCESS: Lecture

1. Actions—Actions are at least as important as words in communicating. The way a person stands or sits, uses his arms and legs, and makes or does not make eye contact can communicate not only the message, but the intent of the speaker. To help create a positive image and to communicate a positive message, every action should be relaxed, open, responsive and attentive. Arms should be relaxed, legs crossed toward the listener, eyes and face showing pleasant expression, and attention keen. Any deviation—legs crossed away from the listener, a frown or grimace, a bored or disinterested look—will undermine even the most positive verbal message.

2. Articulation—The difference between effective and ineffective communication is often articulation. Proper articulation requires good vocal inflection, a clear and understandable rate of speech, a pleasant voice tone, and crisp enunciation.

3. Appearance—Although a speaker can overcome a negative appearance to effectively communicate, an attractive appearance greatly enhances communication. Good posture, whether the speaker is seated or standing, appropriate, neat clothing, and control of distracting mannerisms all combine to provide a positive appearance.

4. Awareness—Although the audience may not be aware of them, effective communication can be enhanced or diminished by many factors. When the speaker is as physically close as possible to the listeners, when he or she pays strict attention to the audience, and when he or she responds quickly to questions and shifts in audience mood, communication effectiveness is enhanced.

5. Appointments—The appointments or setting of a small-group meeting greatly affect nonverbal communications. The size of the room and furnishings should always be appropriate for the small group. Furniture and decorations should enhance communication, not serve as a distraction or barrier (for example, a large centerpiece on a coffee table could inhibit conversation). All participants should sit on the same level, not some on chairs and sofas and others on the floor. Room size should be comfortable, neither cramped nor cavernous. When the room is too large for the audience, people should be moved to its front and middle. In general, a living room or family room setting encourages informal, open communication in a small group better than a classroom setting.

NONVERBAL COMMUNICATION SKILLS

ACTIONS

Facial Expressions
Feet and Legs

ARTICULATION

Inflection
Rate
Tone
Enunciation

APPEARANCE

Posture
Clothing
Mannerisms

AWARENESS

Spacing
Attention
Response

APPOINTMENTS

Room Size
Furnishings

31

COMMUNICATION – INTERACTIONS

OBJECTIVE: Discuss small-group interactions.

TIME: Will vary.

PROCESS:

HEALTHY GROUP
(Characteristics on pages 41 and 42).

1. Discuss a healthy group, in which all members participate in the discussion. Ask a volunteer to share about a healthy group in which he has been a member.

   Questions you might use to aid group discussion:

   What made this group healthy?

   Did you respect the structure (stopping and starting on time, prayer, worship, and Bible study) in the group?

   Did you feel like you helped to make decisions in the group? Did you feel like it was your group?

   Did you grow spiritually as a result of the Bible discussion?

   Was there a sense of belonging and caring for each other?

   Did you feel your opinions and contributions were appreciated?

LEADER-CENTERED GROUP
(Characteristics on page 40).

2. Discuss a leader-centered group and its problems. Ask a volunteer to share about membership in this type of group.

   Questions you might use to aid group discussion:

   How did you feel about participating in a leader-centered group?

   Was there an opportunity to contribute to the discussion?

   Did you feel any ownership in the group?

   Did you want to continue with the group?

   Did you feel "cared for"?

UNHEALTHY GROUP
(Characteristics on page 43).

3. Discuss an unhealthy group. Ask a volunteer to describe what takes place in such a group.

Questions you might use to aid group discussion:

Were you pleased with the level of Bible study that took place?

Was there a strong bonding between the members of the group?

Was there a structure that allowed for prayer, sharing, Bible study, and missions?

Were there people who seemed to dominate the conversation and others who never seemed to join in the discussion?

Did the group start and stop on time?

Summarize by emphasizing that healthy groups help us to reach our goals, while leader-centered or unhealthy groups do not.

HEALTHY GROUP

LEADER-CENTERED GROUP

UNHEALTHY GROUP

32

ASKING QUESTIONS

OBJECTIVE: Learn how to draw people into a discussion with questions.

TIME: Will vary.

PROCESS: Lecture

Draft a plan. A good discussion plan is to use questions to draw people from the general to the specific.

Reach for both information and opinions. "What does the passage say?" "What do you think about that?"

Avoid questions that produce yes or no responses.

Wait. As the leader, don't rush in to answer. Give participants time to answer.

Inspire and encourage. Ask questions first of the group, then of the individual. Create an environment where success is easy.

Name. Call members by name when asking questions.

Give verbal hugs, affirm people. As leader, you will model positive behavior and affirmation. If you are positive, your group will most likely be positive.

One thought at a time. Don't ask overly general questions. Don't ask more than one question at a time.

Use a variety of questions. Three types of questions are knowledge, understanding, and application:

> What does it say?

> What does it mean?

> How does it apply to you?

Transition. Relate information from lesson to lesson. Do not expect people to make giant steps. Build a bridge for understanding.

ASKING QUESTIONS

Asking questions stimulates discussion, draws people out, and directs communication within a group.

D raft a _plan_.

R each for both _information_ and _opinions_.

A void _yes_ or _no_ responses.

W _ait_.

I _nspire_.

N _ame_.

G ive verbal _hugs_, affirm people.

O ne _thought_ at a time.

U se a _variety_ of questions.

T _ransitions_.

ANSWERING QUESTIONS

OBJECTIVE: Recognize the difference in answering questions positively or negatively.

TIME: Will vary.

PROCESS: Lecture

Content. Verify that what you think you have just said is what the person wanted to hear. Ask, "Is that what you wanted to know?"

Look. Look at nonverbal information. Observe nonverbal communication—i.e., eye contact, posture, mannerisms, gesturing, and distancing (how close or far away people stand or sit).

Answer. Answer questions when you can, but if you are unable to answer, say, "I don't know, but I will find out."

Repeat. Repeat the question. This is a compliment to the person asking the question. It implies that you are interested and are listening.

Identify. Identify what is being asked—both the *content* and the *intent*. Listen not only to words but to the thought, depth of feeling, personal meaning, even the meaning that is below the conscious intent of the speaker.

Tact. Use tact in answering questions. Do not make someone feel stupid for asking a question. If you do, that person will probably not speak again and will likely leave the group.

Yield. Do not be the expert. Yield to the group, providing an opportunity for the experience of others in the group to be shared. One good response is "Does anyone else in the group want to respond to this question?"

Do not be negative! Remember, when tension goes up, learning goes down. Review by emphasizing the statements in the box.

ANSWERING QUESTIONS

C ontent

L ook

A nswer

R epeat

I dentify

T act

Y ield

Don't be negative.
Don't be unresponsive.
Don't be a wanderer.
Don't treat two questions as one.

34

SHARING QUESTIONS

OBJECTIVE: Define the need for sharing questions.

TIME: Will vary.

PROCESS: Lecture (paraphrase or read aloud).

A steady diet of superficial conversation can literally strangle the soul. We have been created to relate with God and our fellow man. We long to know and be known at deep personal levels, though we fear that involvement. Simply sitting with a small group of people does not guarantee building personal relationships at a level which allows us to affirm each other. Groups need a structure that will facilitate personal sharing.

"Sharing questions" are those that can be used to prompt in-depth conversations. They are simple one- or two-sentence questions, usually open-ended, which permit and encourage people to talk about themselves. There are no "right" or "wrong" answers; rather, people are encouraged to talk about their past experiences, feelings, hopes for the future, fears and anxieties, their pilgrimage of faith, day-to-day situations, likes and dislikes, sorrows and joys.

Our goal is not to share ideas and concepts, but to share ourselves. This self-disclosure results in our being known, and makes it possible for us to receive affirmation and love. The risk is, if we let people know us, they may not like us. Refusing the risk, however, means refusing to receive the love which we all need so desperately. Sharing questions should encourage, but not force people to share beyond their own willingness.

Explain the following three types of sharing questions: (1) *personal,* (2) *spiritual,* (3) *deeply spiritual.*

As your group develops, sharing questions can play an important role in moving the group from one stage to another. While you are getting to know each other, the *personal* sharing question (How many children do you have? What are their names and ages?) keeps the group in "cliché conversation" (see page 76), the beginning stage of development. Of the four components of small-group life—nurture, worship, community, and missions (see page 109)—the majority of group time is spent in developing relationships.

Spiritual questions help a group begin to share ideas, opinions, and feelings (see page 55). (Do you have a regular time for studying God's Word? If "yes," what difference has it made in your life?) This is the middle stage of a group's development.

Deeply spiritual sharing questions provide the potential to move to peak communication (see page 76), which fosters spiritual growth. Peak communication involves openness, transparency, and self-disclosure. (Has God become "real" to you? When?)

Purposely use these types of sharing questions to help move your group through levels of communication and achieve your goals of getting to know each other, bonding, and reaching people for Christ.

SHARING QUESTIONS

Small groups should be structured in a way that encourages personal sharing. One method is the use of sharing questions. Here are some possible examples:

PERSONAL

What do you like to do for fun?

What would be your ideal vacation?

What was the most memorable thing you did with your family when you were a child?

What quality do you most appreciate in a friend?

How many children do you have? What are their names and ages?

SPIRITUAL

Describe any spiritual milestones that have occurred in your life.

Do you have a regular time for studying God's Word? If "yes," what difference has it made in your life?

If you were asked to define "a Christian," what would you say?

DEEPLY SPIRITUAL

Has God become "real" to you? When?

In what one area of your Christian walk would you most like to grow? What help do you need to accomplish that growth?

Have you done something recently in which your Christian faith made a difference? Explain.

Have you been instrumental in the growth of another person? How?

35

SHARING QUESTION NOTES

OBJECTIVE: Learn why sharing questions are sometimes not successful.

TIME: Will vary.

PROCESS:

1. Have a volunteer go to the flip chart.

2. Ask members of small groups to list obstacles to sharing. Record their responses on the flip chart.

3. Then add obstacles and their results from the following list:

   ◆ A gossip in the group—People are afraid to reveal anything.

   ◆ Leader-centered group—People do not get much chance to talk.

   ◆ Study content too deep—People are at different levels of spiritual development.

   ◆ Intimidation—People will not contribute if an "expert" is present.

   ◆ Group leader not prepared—People do not like to waste their time, they will lose interest in the group and drop out.

   ◆ Lack of interest—People who have personal problems would not be willing to talk about them.

   ◆ Size of group—With more than twelve people, the group becomes a crowd, not an intimate group.

   ◆ Frequency of meeting—If they meet too infrequently, people will not get to know each other.

   ◆ Location and seating arrangement—A classroom arrangement feels formal and focuses on the leader.

   ◆ Time of meeting—People will not talk if they are exhausted or rushed.

   ◆ Fear of rejection—People will not be honest if they know only certain views are accepted.

4. Follow these rules when using sharing questions:

   a. No one talks more than one minute.

   b. Go around the circle.

   c. Do not question people as they share.

SHARING QUESTION NOTES

SMALL-GROUP EXERCISE

OBJECTIVES: Establish a small group.
Understand its components.

TIME: Twenty to twenty-five minutes; give a five-minute warning when time is almost up.

PROCESS:

Instruct the groups to appoint leaders and work through the small-group exercise.

SMALL-GROUP EXERCISE

OPENING

Introduce yourself.

PRAYER

Pair off with a member of your group. Have a moment of conversation, then pray for one another.

SHARING

What one personal relationship would you like to work on? Why? How?

BIBLE STUDY

"We all like sheep have gone astray, each of us have turned to his own way" (Isaiah 53:6).

    a. What does this passage *say* to you?

    b. What does this passage *mean* to you?

    c. How does this passage *apply* to you?

CLOSE

Each member should tell one good thing God has done for you this week; then, pray a prayer of thanks to God for the grace in each life represented. Use the conversational prayer format.

3

WITNESSING

EVERYONE SHOULD BE PREPARED TO WITNESS. ARE YOU?

OBJECTIVE: Identify present strengths and limitations in witnessing skills.

TIME: Four minutes.

PROCESS:

1. Have each participant respond to the questionnaire on page 83.

2. Have each list areas they would like to improve at the bottom of the sheet.

3. Explain that many of these areas will be covered in this training.

EVERYONE SHOULD BE PREPARED TO WITNESS. ARE YOU?

Are you a person with the following?

YES NO
- ❑ ❑ A positive faith attitude
- ❑ ❑ Confidence
- ❑ ❑ Good listening skills
- ❑ ❑ Time spent in prayer

Can you define or quote the following?

YES NO
- ❑ ❑ Characteristics of the nonbeliever
- ❑ ❑ Scriptures for soul-winning
- ❑ ❑ Friendship evangelism

Can you do the following?

YES NO
- ❑ ❑ Share your personal testimony.
- ❑ ❑ Use "bridge" statements in witnessing.
- ❑ ❑ Listen for the need expressed.

Could you answer the following?

YES NO
- ❑ ❑ What are the differences in evangelism from the '60s to the '90s?
- ❑ ❑ How can I use relationships for evangelism?
- ❑ ❑ Define seven steps to effective friendship evangelism.
- ❑ ❑ List eight levels of spiritual development.

Can you use the following as witnessing tools?

YES NO
- ❑ ❑ The Roman Road
- ❑ ❑ Romans 6:23
- ❑ ❑ Four Spiritual Laws

List areas you would like to improve:

40

ESSENTIALS OF WITNESSING

OBJECTIVE: Learn *why* and *how* to reach nonbelievers.

TIME: Will vary.

PROCESS:

1. Mini-lecture, filling in the blanks on pages 85-86.

2. Provide copies of the "Four Spiritual Laws," "The Roman Road," or other witnessing tools, and show how they're used in witnessing. This is an opportune time to have a pastor or minister of evangelism discuss witnessing.

ESSENTIALS OF WITNESSING

KNOW THE CHARACTERISTICS OF THE NONBELIEVER

The nonbeliever is a person _who is spiritually dead_
and _eternally separated_ from God; a person without
hope, and unwilling to give up _sin_.

KNOW THE IMPORTANCE OF SHARING THE GOSPEL

Believe that people want to be saved and that Jesus is the only hope,
the only One who can meet the needs of life. People have the
guilt of sin. People have a _fear of life_
and a _fear of death_. People want to have a
purpose, and a sense of _direction_. People want
to know how to "_get along_" in life.

KNOW HOW TO SHARE YOUR FAITH

Your presentation of the gospel should be _clear_ and
understandable. Using _bridge_ statements can
get you into your presentation. Examples include:

- "Do you think much about spiritual things?"
- "If someone were to ask you 'What is a Christian?' what would
  you say?"
- "Would you mind if I showed you in the Bible what it means to
  become a Christian?"

Effective witnessing tools:

- Four Spiritual Laws—Four-step outline of the plan of salvation,
  published by Campus Crusade.

41

ESSENTIALS OF WITNESSING, continued

- ◆ Romans 6:23—Succinct scriptural explanation of sin's consequences and God's gift of grace.

- ◆ The Roman Road—A progressive outline of the plan of salvation from Romans, published by Baptist General Convention.

USE THE FOLLOWING STATEMENTS AS YOU CLOSE

- ◆ "Would you like to accept Jesus right now?"
- ◆ "Now that you are a Christian, how do you think a Christian ought to live?"

KNOW HOW TO CLOSE

Instruct the new believer in _growing in his faith_ , by studying the Word, spending time in _prayer_ , and becoming involved in a _church_ . Leave relevant _Scriptures_ so the new believer can review. Then close in prayer.

EFFECTIVE COMMUNICATION IN WITNESSING

OBJECTIVE: Understand effective witnessing.

TIME: Eight minutes.

PROCESS:

1. Have each sub-group read pages 88-89.

2. Have them rank the top five in order of importance in witnessing.

3. List the top five from each sub-group on a flip chart, and come up with the overall top five witnessing communication skills. Generally the top five include:

   ◆ Be specific.
   ◆ Know what you want to say.
   ◆ Use a logical sequence.
   ◆ Involve your listener.
   ◆ Follow-up.
   ◆ Be open.
   ◆ Be aware of intent.

   Commend the group by stating that the five they selected are often chosen.

OPTIONAL EXERCISE:

Following this exercise, and depending on the schedule of your small-group skills training, you may wish to have a time of one-on-one witnessing. Use a tool such as "The Roman Road" or "Romans 6:23," but model witnessing to the group before that assignment. Enlist someone to help with this segment, and practice prior to training.

"The Roman Road" is a witnessing tool that uses verses from Romans to take a nonChristian through the plan of salvation: Romans 3:23, 6:23, 5:8, and 10:9-10,13.

By breaking down Romans 6:23—"For the wages of sin is death; but the gift of God is eternal life through Jesus Christ our Lord"—and explaining the meaning of specific words, a person can be led to a life with Christ.

EFFECTIVE COMMUNICATION IN WITNESSING

PRESENT SINGLE IDEAS

Don't throw out a large number of ideas at one time. Encourage reaction and acceptance of an idea once you've presented it.

BE SPECIFIC

Communicate as accurately as possible. The more specific you can be, the better. Use examples, analogies, and illustrations; avoid over-generalizing.

RESPOND TO EMOTIONS

Encourage people to share not only their thoughts but also their feelings, and try to draw feelings out. Express praise, understanding, and appreciation for the other person's feelings. Accept the negative emotions that people may have.

BE OPEN

Be open to giving all you have and all that you know. When you are open, people will be open with you.

KNOW WHAT YOU WANT TO SAY

Make sure that your thoughts and ideas on witnessing—the points that you want to cover—are clear in your mind. If they're not clear to you, it is almost impossible to make them clear to others.

USE A LOGICAL SEQUENCE

Put your thoughts and ideas in a sequence that makes sense to your listeners. It may be chronological; it may be topical; or it may be from more important to less important.

INVOLVE YOUR LISTENER

To reach the minds of your listeners, you need to draw them out. Ask questions. Listen to them as they speak.

GIVE FEEDBACK

When someone says something that can be interpreted several ways, give your interpretation to make sure that it matches their intent.

TAKE THE TOTAL ENVIRONMENT INTO ACCOUNT WHENEVER YOU COMMUNICATE

Be aware of lighting, room arrangement, physical setting, time of day, and the circumstances under which people came to the meeting.

BE AWARE OF INTENT AS WELL AS CONTENT

Your tone of voice, body posture, facial expressions, and openness to the input of others can all communicate the importance of your content and the respect you have for your listener.

FOLLOW-UP

Feedback tells you that your message has been received. Check to make sure you're actually getting your content across. Ask questions. Encourage feedback and input during the conversation.

EFFECTIVE EVANGELISM: THEN AND NOW

OBJECTIVE: Describe the changes in evangelism since the '60s.

TIME: Will vary.

PROCESS: Point out the differences in the '60s and '90s related to effective evangelism.

	THEN '60s	NOW '90s
SOCIAL SETTING	*Post-Industrial* Confrontational; post WWII — if I were to die tonight?	*"High Tech/High Touch"* Now there is stress on *love*, and getting four hugs a day.
SOCIAL COMPLEXITY	*Somewhat Complex* Drug abuse, abortion.	*Highly Complex* No easy answers outside of Jesus Christ.
PERSONAL RELATIONSHIPS	*Confrontational* Riots, saying abusive things, campus demonstrations, TV shows and characters, "All in the Family" and Archie Bunker.	*Relational* TV shows, "Cosby" and "Golden Girls," positive relationships.
ORIENTATION	*Verbal* "Tell the gospel convincingly."	*Visual* A TV generation. "Demonstrate the gospel in concrete terms." You can tell a Christian by his love.
FOCAL POINT	*Decision/Event* This was the climax, but we found we need the fruit that remains.	*Disciple/Process* The decision is still vital, but the road leading to maturity is also important.
PRIMARY QUESTION	"How can I get this person to make a decision for Jesus Christ?"	While this is still primary, now we ask, "In light of this person's pain and hurt, how is Jesus Christ good news to him or her?" Identify the person's need.

EFFECTIVE EVANGELISM: THEN AND NOW

THEN '60s	NOW '90s	
Post-industrial Post-WWII	High-tech High-touch	**SOCIAL SETTING**
Somewhat complex	Highly complex	**SOCIAL COMPLICATIONS**
Confrontational	Relational	**PERSONAL RELATIONSHIPS**
Verbal Tell the gospel convincingly	Visual Demonstrate the gospel in concrete terms.	**ORIENTATION**
Decision/Event	Disciple/Process	**FOCAL POINT**
How can I get this person to make a decision for Jesus Christ?	In light of this person's pain and hurt, how is Jesus Christ good news to him or her?	**PRIMARY QUESTION**

45

EMPLOYING RELATIONSHIPS FOR EVANGELISM

OBJECTIVE: Use relationships in evangelism.

TIME: Will vary.

PROCESS:

Relationship evangelism takes place among our extended family members; that is, family, friends, and coworkers. The following demonstrate the advantages of such an approach. Fill in each blank on page 93, adding the following for each one:

1. The network includes friends, neighbors, and coworkers to whom a person can more easily witness.

2. People tend to have deeper levels of conversation with those whom they have relationships with and trust.

3. On an airplane, for example, there is not sufficient time to get to know someone and when you leave, there is no way to follow-up or offer support.

4. "Oikos" is Greek for *household*. Be available to answer questions and follow-up.

5. Assimilation is possible because you are able to direct the new convert to a church program.

6. God moves through webs of relationships. Many times, when one member of a family has been won to Christ, entire families are won.

7. The law of multiplication. You touch two people, they touch four, the four touch eight, and it continues.

EMPLOYING RELATIONSHIPS FOR EVANGELISM

1. Provide a __natural network__ for sharing the good news of God's redemptive love.

2. Are more likely to involve __receptive__ people.

3. Allow for __unhurried__ and __natural sharing__ of God's love.

4. Provide __natural support__ when the "Oikos" member comes to Christ.

5. Result in the effective __assimilation__ of new converts into the Church.

6. Tend to win entire __families__.

7. Provide a constantly __enlarging__ source of __new contacts__.

EFFECTIVE FRIENDSHIP EVANGELISM—SEVEN STEPS

OBJECTIVE: Identify seven steps of friendship evangelism.

TIME: Will vary.

PROCESS: Lecture

1. Identify your *extended family*. This includes people with whom you have regular contact, whether through kinship (through birth or marriage), friendship, or association, such as coworkers or schoolmates.

   a. Write down the names of members of your extended family who are unchurched or unsaved.

   b. Make a star by the ones with whom you have the most contact.

   c. Turn to page 97. (Leader, follow the instruction.)

   d. When page 98 has been completed, return to this page.

2. Develop a *personal profile* of each extended family member. The sample chart on page 98 can be used to store this information. It is vital to show a healthy interest in each friend or family member, for the more you understand his concerns and interests, the more redemptive your relationship can be. To fight a war requires strategy and as believers, it is important for us to have a strategy for winning people to the Lord. This profile is a beginning point.

3. *Focus* your efforts. Narrow the list to those individuals with whom you have a natural, warm relationship, people you enjoy, and with whom you have a variety of common interests.

4. Develop a *disciple-making plan*. Remember that Christ's approach to people was highly individual. He met people at their point of need, and we should do the same. In this plan, consider the following guidelines:

   a. Care. You are an expression of God's love and care. Moreover, your caring and friendship with others must be unconditional, and not simply the bait of a religious trap.

   b. Take time to strengthen relationships. As you spend time together, your personal sense of values and purpose will naturally emerge. Your greatest resource in developing a meaningful and caring friendship is to simply be yourself, natural and unmasked, with a healthy attitude of, "I'm not perfect, just forgiven." Remember that love is a four-letter word, spelled T-I-M-E.

   c. Use other members of the body. Use the unique resources of your church and other believers. Introduce your extended family member to others in your church; use present church programs, classes, and activities, including church-sponsored social events. Invite other believers, who have interests similar to your extended family member, to spend time with you. Provide him or her with as many different exposures to the gospel as possible.

   d. Share your faith during receptive moments. Be sensitive to the spiritual needs and openness of those in your extended family, and to the leading of the Holy Spirit. Verbalize your belief in

Jesus Christ, and point to specific scriptures when appropriate. When you give your testimony, use words a nonChristian can understand. Realize that evangelism is not complete until a person is discipled and involved in a local church.

e. Be patient. Exercising patience and consistency is crucially important in friendship evangelism, for each person is at a different stage of spiritual growth.

5. Put your disciple-making plan into *action*. Be sensitive and aware of the events in your extended family member's life, for there is a right and wrong time to share, just as there is a right and wrong way to communicate Christ's love. Some suggestions:

a. Listen attentively. Concentrate on what the person is saying, rather than letting your thoughts roam. Put yourself in the other person's place, to see situations from his perspective. Be empathetic, comprehending, and non-judgmental.

b. Relate to needs. Points of need in your own life, or the lives of your extended family members, provide a natural point for demonstrating your Christian faith, relating your experiences, and discussing the solutions Christ has provided you.

c. Identify receptive periods. God's love and caring is especially appropriate during significant life changes, such as marriage, childbirth, a new job or retirement, or during incidents of stress and periods of transition. It is important to stay in touch with your extended family members and respond immediately in time of need.

d. Use appropriate time. *When* you communicate God's love and the Christian faith can be as important as *what* you communicate.

e. Use understandable language. Sharing the realities and benefits of Christ in everyday language lends a credibility and relevance to Christian faith that is important to an unbeliever.

6. *Pray* regularly and specifically for each extended family member. Prayer is at the heart of friendship evangelism. Pray for each person in your extended family on a daily basis, by name, mentioning specific needs and situations.

7. Accept your *accountability* to others and to God. A final step in effective friendship evangelism is to meet regularly with other Christians who are involved in this process. Praying together and sharing goals and experiences in regular meetings provides an important source of support, fellowship, and accountability. Commitment to regular prayer partners is a vital link in a chain of relationships that bring many into the Master's Kingdom. We are accountable to God to win other people to Jesus Christ, and we should also be accountable to one another.

EFFECTIVE FRIENDSHIP EVANGELISM—SEVEN STEPS

1. Identify your __extended family__.

2. Develop a __personal profile__ of each extended family member.

3. __Focus__ your efforts.

4. Develop a __disciple-making__ plan.
   a. Care.
   b. Take time to strengthen relationships.
   c. Use other members of the Body.
   d. Share your faith during receptive moments.
   e. Be patient.
   f. Trust the Holy Spirit.

5. Put your disciple-making plan into __action__.
   a. Listen attentively.
   b. Relate to needs.
   c. Identify receptive periods.
   d. Use appropriate time.
   e. Use understandable language.

6. __Pray__ regularly and specifically for each extended family member.

7. Accept your __accountability__ to God and to others.

EXTENDED FAMILY MEMBER—PERSONAL PROFILE

OBJECTIVE: Write a personal profile.

TIME: Will vary.

PROCESS:

1. Explain the form by walking through each section.

2. Now have each member of the class fill out the form, using the name of one of the people they "starred."

3. When they have completed the form, ask if they were surprised at the information they knew or did not know about this person.

4. Return to page 94, pick up at number 2.

EXTENDED FAMILY MEMBER—PERSONAL PROFILE

Name _____ Birthday _____

Address _____

Home Phone _____ Work Phone _____

Place of Employment _____

Occupation _____

Personal Background

Exposure to Christian Faith and Life

Hobbies and Interests

Family Life and Expressed Degree of Satisfaction

Job Satisfaction

Current Events in Life

Knowledge of Bible; Degree of Openness to Discussing Spiritual
Matters; Reason(s) Not Currently a Believer

48

EIGHT LEVELS OF SPIRITUAL DEVELOPMENT

OBJECTIVE: Identify the levels of spiritual development.

TIME: Five minutes (sub-group time).

PROCESS:

1. Mini-lecture: the "Eight Levels of Spiritual Development."

   While presenting the eight levels, mention the Scriptures in the margin. You may ask group members to read them aloud.

   Every lost person needs to hear the Word of God through the witness of a believer. Each one is a unique being with a distinct personality. Each person is at a different level of spiritual development.

   Some approaches in witnessing are message-centered. Their aim is to present the message of the gospel. If the unbeliever is under conviction and ready to receive Christ, this is an excellent approach. But if not, another approach should be taken.

   A person-centered approach might be better. A witness for Christ needs to be perceptive to the level of spiritual development of the lost person.

   A witness for Christ should learn to introduce Christ at the point of a person's need, regardless of that person's level of spiritual development.

2. Have each sub-group review the eight levels of spiritual development, and discuss people they know who may fit in one of these levels. (Five minutes)

3. Ask the entire group if they are able to identify people they have known who are at any of these levels. If so, have at least two people tell how they would approach that person now.

EIGHT LEVELS OF SPIRITUAL DEVELOPMENT

A witness for Christ should learn to introduce Christ at the point of a person's need, regardless of that person's level of spiritual development.

There are two classes of people in the world — believers and non-believers (see John 3:18).

NONBELIEVERS

INDIFFERENCE LEVEL
Needs to be stirred. The Word of God stirs through the conviction of the Holy Spirit. The boat must be rocked for change to come.

Hebrews 4:12

HOSTILITY LEVEL
Needs to be loved. It is hard to love a bitter person. Only through Christ, exercising God's love, can one love the unlovely. He needs someone to love him enough to listen, to help him work through hostility, and to express Christ's concern for him.

Matthew 5:43-44
Mark 2:17

IGNORANCE LEVEL
Needs to be taught. Sow the seed of the Word. Instruct.

Ephesians 2:1-5
Romans 10:17

INTEREST LEVEL
Needs to be cultivated. Continue to sow the seed of the Word. The Holy Spirit does the cultivating.

John 6:44

CONVICTION LEVEL
Needs to be guided to Christ. Explain that Jesus loves him and died for him, though this person has sinned.

Acts 8:31
Romans 5:8

CONVERSION LEVEL
Needs to be led to the Cross. Encourage the person to confess with his mouth what he believes.

Romans 10:9-10

BELIEVERS

GROWING LEVEL
Needs to be encouraged and taught.

Ephesians 4:12-15

BACKSLIDING LEVEL
Needs to be confronted, loved, and restored.

Jeremiah 2:19
Galatians 6:1-2

SMALL-GROUP EXERCISE

OBJECTIVES: Establish a small group.
Understand its components.

TIME: Twenty to twenty-five minutes; give a five-minute warning when time is almost up.

PROCESS:

1. Instruct each sub-group to appoint a leader and to work through the small-group exercise.

2. If time permits, have the participants fill out "Eyes for My Community" (pages 104-105). If not, make it a homework assignment. Whether the form is filled out in class or out of class, be sure to discuss the responses.

SMALL-GROUP EXERCISE

OPENING

Introduce yourself.

PRAYER

Begin with a "burden bearer's prayer," in which a request is given, then immediately prayed for by another member in the group.

SHARING

Briefly tell when and how you became a Christian.

BIBLE STUDY

Here are a series of questions concerning believers. Before answering, take turns reading (out loud) the appropriate scriptures.

    a. How does one become a believer? (John 11:25-26, Acts 16:30-31)

    b. What are the marks of a believer? (Matthew 16:24; John 8:31-32, 13:12-15)

    c. What does a disciple do? (Matthew 28:18-20, Mark 5:18-20; John 15:8, 1 Peter 3:15)

    d. What are two characteristics of a disciple? (John 8:12, 13:35)

    e. What is a modern-day disciple?

CLOSE

Close with conversational prayer.

ASSIGNMENT

Complete "Eyes for My Community," then discuss what you wrote, and find out how others in the group responded.

EYES FOR MY COMMUNITY

OBJECTIVE: To broaden the vision for small groups.

TIME: Five minutes to complete the form; five minutes to share in large group.

PROCESS:

1. Have each participant complete the form, "Eyes for My Community."

2. In the large group, have several people share their "vision."

3. Close the "Witnessing" session in prayer or song.

EYES FOR MY COMMUNITY

"Community" can be defined in one of two ways: (1) those in your geographical area; or (2) those with whom you work or best relate. Before starting this, decide which definition you desire.

1. DESCRIBE
   Take a few moments and briefly describe your community.
   Include such items as general location:

   Approximate number of people:

   Approximate ages of people:

   Approximate percentage of churched and unchurched:

   Occupations represented:

   Any distinctive characteristics:

2. ASSESS NEEDS
   From what you know at this point, if you were to ask the members of your community what they considered their community's three greatest needs, what would they say? Be as specific as possible.

   a.

   b.

   c.

3. SEE THROUGH GOD'S EYES
   If God freely did anything in your community that He wanted to do in the next year, what changes do you think you would see by the end of that year? In short, what do you think God's vision is for your community?

   a.

   b.

   c.

51

4. YOUR ROLE
   Considering what you know about your community, and what you sense God wants to do, what two specific things could you do to help bring this vision about?

   a.

   b.

   What two specific things could your group do?

   a.

   b.

4

RELATIONSHIPS

COMPONENTS OF SMALL-GROUP LIFE

OBJECTIVE: Describe and discuss four components of small-group life.

TIME: Five minutes (sub-group time).

PROCESS:

1. Explain: The four components of small-group life—nurture, worship, community, and missions—are vital to a healthy group. If a group develops an apathetic feeling and doesn't seem to grow, find out if the four components are all present in the group's life.

2. Review the four components and the definition, goal, and examples of activities under each component. Make sure everyone understands each item.

3. Have each sub-group discuss a particular mission project that could be implemented by their group (examples: write a missionary, adopt a needy family). Remember that it's tempting to ignore mission when you are just starting a group.

COMPONENTS OF SMALL-GROUP LIFE

COMPONENTS	NURTURE	WORSHIP	COMMUNITY	MISSION
DEFINITION	Being fed by God to grow like Christ.	Praising and magnifying God by focusing on His nature, action, and words.	Fellowship centered around the experience we share as Christians.	Reaching out with the good news of Christ's love to people in need.
GOAL	To become like Jesus.	To bring joy to God.	To knit us together in love and build us as whole people.	To help people know God and become like Jesus.
EXAMPLES OF ACTIVITIES	◆ Discussing the Bible, books, tapes, lectures ◆ Memorizing Scripture ◆ Testimonies	◆ Praying ◆ Singing ◆ Reading worshipful passages from the Bible or books ◆ Kneeling	◆ Praying with prayer partners ◆ Bearing each other's burdens ◆ Eating together ◆ Helping each other develop gifts ◆ Intercession	◆ Praying for nonChristian friends or unreached people ◆ Sharing the gospel with a specific group of unbelievers ◆ Raising money for world hunger relief

COVENANT

OBJECTIVE: Establish a covenant.

TIME: Will vary.

PROCESS:

1. Define *covenant*: an agreement among group members, concerning both the group's purpose and its methods for achieving that purpose.

2. Explain why a group may choose to covenant.

   A free-flowing group can be undisciplined and ineffective; a covenant clarifies their purpose. Because group members know what they are getting into from the beginning, there are fewer disappointments and conflicts later on. In the event problems arise, the covenant can be used to solve them. Often a commitment will provide the strength to continue when things get tough. A covenant agreed upon by all gives ownership to all members, and guards against a leader-centered group.

3. Pray before the meeting when the covenant will be made. This meeting can be a great strength to the group and enhance its growth.

4. Forms may vary; use the one on the next page, or develop your own.

5. A part of the covenant is to develop a meeting format. The sample leadership manual includes a typical meeting format on page 173 and a blank form, which can allow the group to decide on its own format. Make copies of the typical meeting format and the covenant available for use by the leaders and participants in their covenanting meeting.

6. Review the form on the next page line by line.

7. Turn to pages 123 and 124 and review item 6 (recognition of the stages of a group's life). Indicate that the differentiation and change stage (e) is the time for a group to discuss new curriculum and re-covenant to bring new life to the group.

COVENANT

LEADER _Sue Smith_

SCHEDULE

Meeting time

   start _9 a.m._

   stop _11 a.m._

Meeting day _Tuesday_

Meeting place

1500 Spring Road
Dallas, TX 75240

TYPICAL MEETING FORMAT

Fellowship
Prayer / Worship
Bible study
   discussion

HOST/HOSTESS _Carol Jones_

DETAILS

Refreshments _coffee & cookies_

Children _at the church_

Absences _call & send cards_

Bible version _NIV_

Curriculum _church_

Visitors _welcome – open group_

New members _welcome_

Evaluation _at end of curriculum_

Other _covenant is_
for seven weeks,
the length of the
curriculum

DISCIPLINES

☑ Nurture
   preparation
   attendance
   participation

☑ Worship
   singing
   prayer

☑ Community
   accountability
   confidentiality
   using gifts

☑ Mission
   identify
   pray specifically
   action

"Let us consider how to stir up one another to love and good works" (Hebrews 10:24).

SIGNED
Sue Smith

55

THINGS THAT "CHOKE" A GROUP

OBJECTIVE: List ten things that choke a group.

TIME: Will vary.

PROCESS:

1. Explain: As part of a small group, we have experienced many things that choke the life from a group. To be able to recognize these chokers is the first step to overcoming them.

2. Have a volunteer go to the flip chart and write down chokers mentioned by the large group.

3. Add to the list the following chokers, which haven't been mentioned:

   Spiritual smugness

   Betraying confidences

   Overextending quitting time

   Lack of love and encouragement from the leader

   Lack of child care when needed

   No clearly defined purpose

   Autocratic leadership

   Becoming only a social event

   No leadership—or an unprepared leader

   Location and time not convenient

   Homogeneous population—lack of diversity

   Physical setting too large, cold, and formal

   Repeated lateness or absenteeism

   Focusing on absent members instead of those present

   Being negative and critical of others

THINGS THAT "CHOKE" A GROUP

OVERCOMING COMMON PROBLEMS

OBJECTIVE: Understand common problems.

TIME: Will vary.

PROCESS: Lecture

Some of the skills needed in effective home-group meetings involve problem-solving. Every group has problems. Some common ones, with possible solutions, are:

1. A member who will not participate. Try to involve him in conversation. Find out about his personal involvements, and listen with interest to what he says. Devote some time to him outside your regular meeting, one-on-one. When he does take part in the group, make a special note of it: "That's a good point, Paul. I appreciate your input." Give this person eye contact.

2. A member who is argumentative and obstinate. Keep your temper, and do not let the group get tense and excited. Examine what he says carefully, and try to find the good in it. You might privately explain to him that his view is important, but that he must not destroy the group's effectiveness by his insistence. Visit one-on-one and find out if there is a personal problem.

3. The group is confused, and complains they have been wasting time. Provide agendas and systematic approaches to discussion. Make sure a clear, constructive purpose is fulfilled at each meeting.

4. Group apathy. Find out if you have overlooked any important aspects of the group's life together. Remember the four components: worship, nurture, community, and mission. Check to see if any of the four are missing. Display enthusiasm and energy until it is caught by the group.

5. A group that is resistant, antagonistic, or hostile. Analyze members' abilities. Assess the most useful role for each member, and support members who assume suitable roles. Remind the group of their purpose. Be creative in using people's gifts.

6. The presence of conflict. There are seven steps to take in dealing with conflict:

   a. Confront the conflict when it is small, instead of waiting until it grows larger.

   b. Try to deal with issues and not personalities.

   c. Recognize others' feelings and concerns.

   d. Focus on facts instead of what someone is attempting to manipulate.

   e. Maintain a trusting and friendly attitude.

   f. Clarify whether one or several issues must be dealt with, and deal with one issue at a time.

   g. Have all parties in the conflict at one meeting (not necessarily a home-group meeting), and reason with all. Pray prior to this meeting. Often, if there is no prayer prior to such a confrontation, it will turn to criticism, gossip or judgment.

7. Handling interruptions. Anticipate interruptions, and plan the meeting in such a way as to minimize them. When interruptions do occur, give them simple recognition, and go on. Remember, not all interruptions are bad; some might represent opportunities for learning. An example of a divine interruption may be a phone call telling of a member of the group in the hospital. Pray for the need.

8. A bad idea is given. Never totally reject any idea. Try to isolate the negative and explore the good in the idea. Affirm the idea-giver, even though you might not fully agree with the idea. Don't ever tell someone they are stupid. If you do, trust will be totally destroyed and no one else will speak. You might say, "That's interesting. What do the rest of you think?" The group will have soft ways to deal with the idea. "That's interesting" is a neutral statement.

OVERCOMING COMMON PROBLEMS

1. A member who will not _participate_.

2. A member who is _argumentative_.

3. The group is _confused_, and complains they have been _wasting time_.

4. Group _apathy_.

5. A group that is _resistant_, _antagonistic_, and _hostile_.

6. The presence of _conflict_.

7. Handling _interruptions_.

8. A _bad idea_ is given.

CLEVER "BEES" MAKE A SUCCESSFUL GROUP

OBJECTIVE: Exhibit leadership characteristics.

TIME: Will vary.

PROCESS: Lecture

1. *Be thoroughly prepared.* The vast majority of Americans expect poor service. In our small groups and our church, we must display excellence. Be prepared!

2. *Be available.* Be available before and after the class, and during the week, as needs arise.

3. *Believe.* Display a strong faith. Show others how God has worked in your life, and be able to direct them to Scripture.

4. *Be understanding.* Participants come to a group with different needs and at different stages of spiritual and emotional growth. Recognize the differences and respond accordingly.

    This is a fun exercise to illustrate differences in needs. On the flip chart, draw a picture of a tree, a man, a child, a bird, and a dog. Then, ask members to answer the following:

    a. What would a man who was an architect use this tree for?

    b. What would a little boy use the tree for?

    c. What would a bird use the tree for?

    d. What would a dog use the tree for?

    After you have a good laugh, stress that everyone has different needs.

5. *Be relevant.* People are looking for application of what they learn to their life. How will this group help each member? Outline and emphasize the benefits of being a member of a small group.

6. *Be an encourager.* Build people up in the Lord. Be affirming. Remember that people walk around carrying a sign that reads "Make Me Feel Important." As leader, you will set the tone for the whole group; if you are a good model, others will follow your lead (1 Corinthians 14:12).

7. *Be resistant to gossip.*

    "And I say to you, that every careless word that men shall speak, they shall render account for it in the day of judgment." (Matthew 12:36)

    Let no unwholesome word proceed from your mouth, but only such a word as is good for edification according to the need of the moment, that it may give grace to those who hear. (Ephesians 4:29)

8. *Be a learner.* Leaders must be learners. You must attend training, read relevant recommended materials, and share what works and doesn't work with other leaders.

9. *Be flexible.* There will be exceptions to all rules. Schedules may have to be adjusted to meet the needs of the group and the church. For example, during a revival at your church, your group may not meet, but instead attend the revival, sit together, and bring friends.

10. *Be dedicated to follow-up.* Follow-up adds depth to your group. Many people are lonely, hurting, and are dealing with tough issues alone. Regular personal contact will reflect a caring leader who models the Christian life.

CLEVER "BEES" MAKE A SUCCESSFUL GROUP

Be thoroughly prepared

Be available

Believe

Be understanding of needs

Be relevant

Be an encourager

Be resistant to gossip

Be a learner

Be flexible

Be dedicated to follow-up

CALLS AND CARDS

OBJECTIVE: State five methods of follow-up.

TIME: Will vary.

PROCESS:

1. Have all participants who have won a potato come to the front of the room.

2. Hand a straw to each of them.

   PURPOSE: The purpose of the potato and straw exercise is to have fun and to visually describe the importance of follow-up or follow-through in a small group. Leaders of small groups are sometimes overtaken with responsibilities and dwell on obstacles. Do not see the potato as an obstacle; rather, equate taking smooth swings with the straw with smooth swings in our groups—keeping a family information form on each participant, keeping a prayer journal, making phone calls, sending cards and letters, and making personal visits. When the straw goes through the potato, stress the point of not seeing the obstacles but *being faithful* to your position in leadership.

3. Show the people how to take a smooth swing, with a smooth follow-through, holding the potato between their thumb and forefinger. Doing this, you can put the straw through the potato. Then, let them do it.

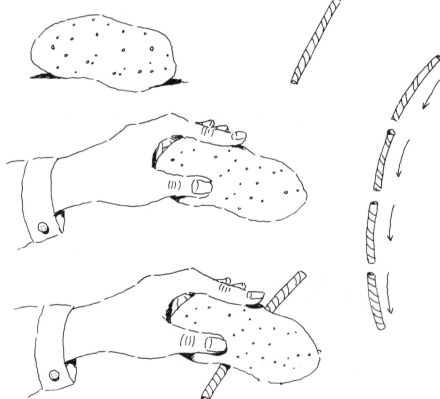

4. Let others come up and try.

5. Discuss the five methods of follow-up.

   a. Family information. A form must be kept to let us know as much about each member as possible, so when a crisis or need arises we are ready. Refer to the participant information form, which gives family information, found on page 181.

   b. Prayer journal. Keeping a record of prayer requests allows you to be updated on a need in a contact's life. It also allows you to share a victory with your group when prayer is answered. Show several sample prayer journals, which can be purchased at any Christian bookstore. These make excellent incentive give-aways in training.

   c. Phone calls. We all want people to like us, to care for and encourage us. Try to call members of your group just to see how they are. Call when things are going well, and when they are not. If you cannot make all the calls, appoint someone in the group to help.

   d. Cards and letters. When a member is absent, cards or letters can be a real encouragement. It is fun to bring a card to the small group meeting and have all the members sign it.

   e. Personal visits. When a member of your group is sick, has a family crisis, or has another type of need, make a personal visit if possible.

> Be shepherds of God's flock that is under your care, serving as overseers—not because you must, but because you are willing, as God wants you to be; not greedy for money, but eager to serve; not lording it over those entrusted to you, but being examples to the flock. And when the Chief Shepherd appears, you will receive the crown of glory that will never fade away. (1 Peter 5:2-4)

CALLS AND CARDS

Family Information Form

Prayer Journal

Phone Calls

Cards and Letters

Personal Visits

CONDUCTING A SMALL-GROUP MEETING

OBJECTIVE: Lead a small-group meeting.

TIME: Will vary.

PROCESS: Lecture

1. Use *sharing questions*. Before the Bible study portion of the meeting, it is helpful to ask sharing questions, which aid in building relationships by permitting people to talk about themselves. In addition to the types of sharing questions discussed on page 75, affirmation questions are excellent for groups to use prior to holidays and vacations, or when a group has decided not to continue meeting. For example:

   ◆ What is one quality you value or admire in one member of this group?

   ◆ If you could give a special gift to each member of the group, what would it be and why?

   ◆ What spiritual gifts do you see present in one member of this group?

   ◆ How are those gifts being used in a helpful way?

   ◆ What has been meaningful to you in this group?

   ◆ How has this group been important or helpful to you?

   ◆ What do you value especially about this group?

   ◆ If you were called on to give a speech describing the good qualities of the members of this group, what would you say?

   These are questions which invite group members to say positive things about each other. Often we form friendships which are meaningful to us, but we seldom say aloud just what our friends mean to us and why we value them. While group members are often reticent to say positive things about each other, it is a quality that can often be seen in the life of Jesus and the apostles. They could see and affirm qualities in people thus helping people to recognize and value what God was doing within and through them. This type of affirmation can be very important in expressing feelings and building a sense of belonging and caring.

2. *Recognize* that each member of the group has a part to play. Never do anything that group members can do themselves. A good leader guides the group with a firm vision of important goals, while allowing members the freedom and creativity necessary for growth (see page 125).

3. *Stop – look – listen.* "Stop" on time. "Look" at the group's reactions. "Listen" to who dominates the conversation.

4. Use *humor* effectively. Natural humor builds cohesion and breaks tension. Try a humorous history-giving exercise, to which members bring old photos of themselves.

5. Be *creative*. Use creativity in planning all areas of group activities. For example, place an empty chair to symbolize a person the group wants to win to Christ. Pray for a person you would like to occupy that chair.

6. Recognize the *stages* of a group's growth. Recognition of the group's current stage will clearly benefit the leadership. The stages are:

   a. Pre-contract stage, as the members are first invited to participate.

   b. Orientation stage, a time of attraction and/or repulsion.

   c. Power and control stage, finding one's particular role.

   d. Trust stage, a time of belonging and unity.

   e. Differentiation and change stage, wanting something new or different.

   f. Conclusion or new beginning.

7. Recognize the *roles* various members play. Recognizing roles facilitates problem-solving and understanding the dynamics of the group. People-oriented roles include: the advocate, who encourages others; the tension reliever, who relieves tension by joke-telling or directing attention from a tense subject. Task-oriented roles include: the clock watcher, who makes sure everything is done properly and on time; the summarizer, who reminds the group where it has been; the energizer, who stimulates others to work toward a goal.
   There are several roles that the leader should actively encourage:

   ◆ An encourager brings others into the discussion, encouraging them to contribute, emphasizing the value of their comments with approval and recognition.

   ◆ A clarifier handles confusion and conflict by defining the problem concisely and pointing out the issues clearly.

   ◆ An explorer is never satisfied with the obvious or traditional, but is always moving into new and different areas.

   ◆ An analyzer examines the issues closely, carefully weighing suggestions, and never accepts anything without thorough thought.

   ◆ A mediator facilitates agreement or harmony between members, finding compromises acceptable to all.

   ◆ A synthesizer is able to put the pieces of thought, opinion, and planning together and synthesize them.

   ◆ A programmer is adept at organizing and moving into action.

CONDUCTING A SMALL-GROUP MEETING

1. Use _personal questions_ .

2. _Recognize_ that each member of the group has a part to play.

3. _Stop_ - _look_ - _listen_ .

4. Use _humor_ effectively.

5. Be _creative_ .

6. Recognize the _stages_ of a group's growth.

7. Recognize the _roles_ various members play.

WHEN AT ALL POSSIBLE — COMMISSION OTHERS

OBJECTIVE: Develop and fill leadership positions.

TIME: Will vary.

PROCESS:

1. Explain: A good leader knows how to develop leadership. Only when each member of your group buys into group ownership will he or she truly feel he or she belongs. It will take time to get acquainted with members of your group, perhaps as long as two months. Always be on the look-out for a gifted person. For instance, call on a natural singer to lead singing, or ask if anyone will serve as worship leader for the group. Continue this process until you have appointed all to positions of leadership. Some members may have more unusual talents. If you have an amateur photographer, let him serve as your small-group photographer, and create a scrapbook. Be flexible. Don't be confined by job descriptions.

2. List the different leadership positions within the pie on page 127.

3. Fill in the numbered items in the margins.

   Question 1: Observe and *identify group members' gifts*.

   Question 2: *Review job descriptions* found in the leadership manual on pages 167-172. Give highlights of each job.

   Question 3: *Encourage* group members to make *a commitment*.

   Question 4: *Pray together*.

> Now the body is not made up of one part, but many. (1 Corinthians 12:14)

WHEN AT ALL POSSIBLE—COMMISSION OTHERS

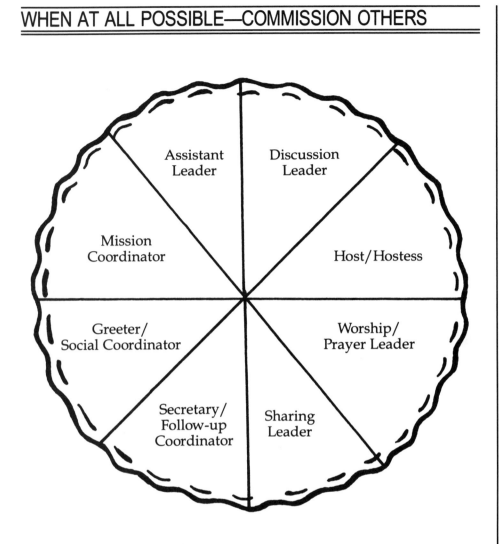

1. *Identify group members' gifts* .
2. *Review job descriptions* .
3. *Encourage a commitment* .
4. *Pray together* .

COMPOSITION OF A SUCCESSFUL BIBLE STUDY

OBJECTIVES: Understand the components of a successful Bible study.
Identify four types of learners.

TIME: Will vary.

PROCESS: Lecture

1. *Pray.* Pray for people in your group every day. Post their names where you can see them regularly, on your bathroom mirror, or car dashboard. Leaders should intercede in prayer for those under their care, and pray also for God's guidance. (See Ephesians 6:18-20.)

2. *List needs.* List both general and specific needs of group members. Your prayer diary and family information sheets can be very helpful. Each person's expectations, needs, or reasons for attending may be different. Be prepared by knowing this in advance.

3. *Research.* Always collect more information than you plan to use when you lead the Bible discussion. If you are using a published Bible study guide, work through the lesson without the aid of the leader's notes to understand problems members might encounter.

4. *Know the material.* Be flexible with the lesson, and do not expect a single response to a question. Allow participants freedom to explore the material, and you be the guide, not the expert. Thorough knowledge will help you keep the group on track, confirming responses with appreciation and affirmation, and generally directing the discussion. (See Titus 2:7-8.)

5. *Realize there are different types of learners.* We assume others learn as we do, but that is not necessarily true. There are four types of learners. Your challenge is to motivate the types found in your group. The four types are: *what, why, how,* and *results* learners.

    a. The *what* learner's primary concern is for information. He likes memorizing, word studies, and working with concordances. While these activities would bore others, they motivate the *what* learner. Give this learner an assignment to research a passage of Scripture or do a word study.

    b. The *why* learner's primary concern is personal meaning. He likes to be personally involved, to interact with others, listening and sharing. Discussing God's Word with others motivates this person.

    c. The *how* learner's primary concern is application. How does it work, and how can it be applied? He likes to try things for himself. When you study a parable (for example, with an emphasis on loving your neighbor), he says, "All right, how do I do that?"

    d. The *results* learner's primary concern is action. He is interested in the results, once something has been applied. You, as leader, need to offer results. For example: "If you apply this principle in your life . . . then. . . ."

Read the Scripture:

"Now finish the work, so that your eager willingness to do it may be matched by your completion of it, according to your means." (2 Corinthians 8:11, NIV)

COMPOSITION OF A SUCCESSFUL BIBLE STUDY

Prior preparation is vital to the success of a Bible study. An effective leader prepares by:

Praying

Listing needs

Researching

Knowing the material

Realizing there are different types of learners

> Now finish the work, so that your eager willing-
> ness to do it may be matched by your completion
> of it, according to your means.
> (2 Corinthians 8:11, NIV)

FIVE-FINGER PRAYER

OBJECTIVE: Conduct a five-finger prayer.

TIME: Will vary.

PROCESS:

1. Review the five-finger diagram, explaining the prayer opportunity each finger represents.

2. Rotate through each sub-group, with the first person touching his thumb and offering a brief conversational prayer, the second person touching his index finger and praying, the third using the middle finger. Continue using the fingers again if more than five are in a particular sub-group.

FIVE-FINGER PRAYER

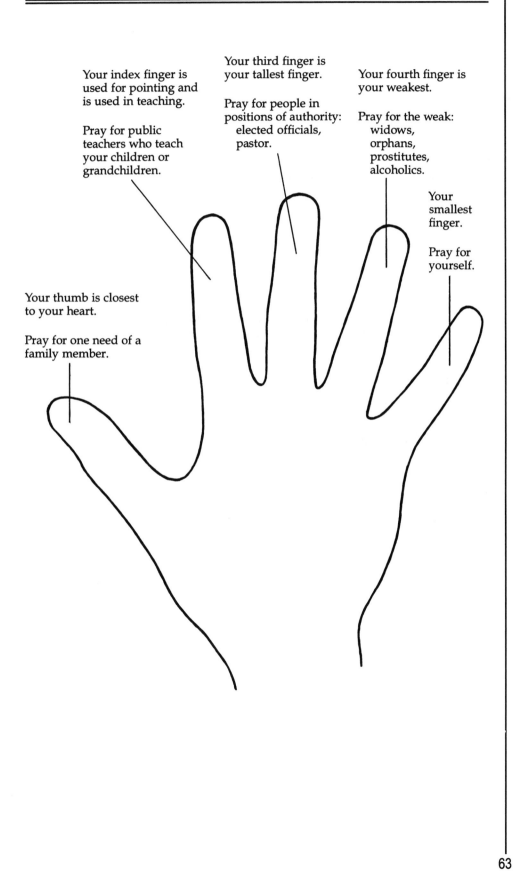

Your index finger is used for pointing and is used in teaching.

Pray for public teachers who teach your children or grandchildren.

Your third finger is your tallest finger.

Pray for people in positions of authority: elected officials, pastor.

Your fourth finger is your weakest.

Pray for the weak: widows, orphans, prostitutes, alcoholics.

Your smallest finger.

Pray for yourself.

Your thumb is closest to your heart.

Pray for one need of a family member.

CASE STUDIES

OBJECTIVE: Handle uncomfortable situations.

TIME: Five minutes (sub-group time).

PROCESS:
1. We have covered a good deal of information. Now let us see how we would solve the following case studies, using our experience from this training as well as our experiences in life.
2. Divide into sub-groups of five, and have each small group select a leader.

3. Assign questions to the groups. To group 1, questions 1-3; group 2, questions 4-6; group 3, questions 7-9; and so on until all the questions have been assigned. The number you assign per group will depend on the number of groups you have in a particular training session.

4. Reconvene the large group and have each sub-group share the responses to their questions, giving people time to record all responses. (Do not use the flip chart this time.)

5. Commend the group as a whole for the knowledge they have acquired and encourage them to continue reading and sharing information with one another. This can continue in your regular leadership meetings.

6. If you need them, sample responses from other training sessions are listed.

SAMPLE RESPONSES TO CASE STUDIES
1. Start on time, no matter what. Begin in prayer. When more of your group is present, explain the need to begin on time. Go back and review the covenant. You may need to change the time or day you meet.

2. Briefly acknowledge, then continue.

3. That person is insecure and has low self-esteem. Model openness and vulnerability and perhaps this will catch on. Treat him or her like other people. Do not allow this person to dominate the conversation.

4. Seize the great opportunity that you have to develop a relationship. Be sensitive to the nonbeliever. Don't overload with Christian jargon. Make the lesson application-oriented. Meet with Christians and have them help you.

5. Clarify. Ask questions to make sure everyone understands a point before moving ahead.

6. Rephrase the question. Give the group time to think of an answer. If there is still no response, answer the question yourself.

7. Briefly comment, then use the time as an opportunity to share the gospel after the meeting.

8. Prompt the group to respond. Lead the group into a discussion of what they agree on, and warn against "passing judgment on disputable matters" (Romans 14:1, NIV).

9. Be honest. Disarm the situation by admitting your weakness. Have a helper lead, if necessary.

10. Affirm their attempt to contribute, then get the group to respond. Point out Scripture that clarifies the correct answer.

11. This may be a trap; do not get off track. Ask, "Why did you ask that question?" Then, build a future study around that question or agree to discuss it further in private.

12. Ask the group why they find it so difficult to keep on track. Re-evaluate the relevance of your curriculum. Create an outline and follow it carefully.

13. Accept and acknowledge her discomfort but don't get sidetracked into a detailed discussion. Offer to discuss it further at a later time, in private.

14. Use body language. Don't make eye contact. Sit next to the person. Visit after the session. Redirect questions. Change seating in the group. Give the talkative member an assignment.

15. Ask the chatting members to respond to a question. Call them by name, and ask a question. If the problem persists, address the issue privately after the meeting.

16. Ask them, "Do you have anything to add?" Talk to the person after the meeting. There may be something in their personal life that is bothering them.

17. If needs are being met, continue.

18. Establish one-on-one contact, and build a loving and trusting relationship. Express interest by continuing to invite the person to the group.

19. Plan your curriculum to meet the needs of *all* group members. Pair new Christians with seasoned Christians for discipling.

20. Divide the group into prayer partners, and always have a support person lead. You may need to consider starting a new group.

21. Invite these new Christians to attend a small group. Follow up with a phone call and personal visit. Ask them to go to church with you.

22. Remember, "Where two or three are gathered . . ." (Matthew 18:20).

CASE STUDIES

WHAT WOULD YOU DO IF . . .

1. It is time to begin, and no more than half your expected group is present.

2. Group members arrive after your discussion is already underway.

3. A Christian in your group displays a superior attitude.

4. Your newly organized group includes five nonbelievers and eight believers.

5. After you have finished discussing a question, you notice some puzzled expressions.

6. You have asked the group a question, and there is no response.

7. A nonChristian begins to ask some questions in the group setting about man's relationship to Christ.

8. A group member insists on the truth and importance of a particular church doctrine or practice.

9. You cannot control your nerves.

10. Someone gives an absolutely incorrect answer.

11. You are studying a passage on marriage, and someone in the group asks how you feel about divorcees remarrying.

CASE STUDIES, continued

12. The group constantly goes off on tangents instead of following the curriculum.

13. Someone is very uncomfortable with the Bible's teaching on a wife's relationship to her husband.

14. One of the members talks on every issue.

15. Several group members bother others by continuing a private discussion.

16. Someone who is obviously prepared for the study does not share in the group discussion.

17. In the middle of a lively and fruitful discussion, you realize you have only three minutes left and another question.

18. A person who has been defensive about his or her religious beliefs drops out.

19. New Christians ask for opportunities for spiritual growth and sharing.

20. You cannot give group members enough time and attention.

21. New Christians from the group are beginning to come to church, but say they do not feel welcome.

22. You want to spin off a new group from the existing one, but you only have two current members interested.

5

PROMOTION AND REVIEW

STARTING A NEW GROUP

OBJECTIVE: Start a new group.

TIME: Will vary.

PROCESS: Review the points of starting a new group.

1. Leadership training: You have completed the first step in starting a new group. I congratulate you.

2. Develop a prospect list of people who may be interested in being a part of a new group. Your list will include friends, neighbors, coworkers, and church members.

3. Identify the target group. Target a group from your prospect list. (It may be a mixture of those you have listed.) Then, list this group's needs and interests. This step will help you choose curriculum which will appeal to the target group.

4. Get down to basics. A contract, verbal, or written, between the small-group leader and each host will outline options, give direction, and provide a starting point, as the host and members decide what type of group they will form.

5. Publicize the new group. Make your invitations personal; one-on-one contact is always the best way to promote your group. It will be necessary to communicate more than once, since people tend to forget times and locations. When promoting your group, dwell on the benefits of participation: meeting new friends, sharing needs with others, belonging to a prayer group, and studying the Word.

6. Pray. As Jesus said, "Ask, and it shall be given to you; seek, and you shall find; knock, and it shall be opened to you" (Matthew 7:7). Ask God daily to send people to your group. Be open to the Holy Spirit's leading when you are around people in conversation. Be aware that everyone is a potential member.

STARTING A NEW GROUP

1. IN LEADERSHIP TRAINING, MAKE SURE YOU'VE DEVELOPED

- Basic leadership skills and gifts
- A teachable spirit
- A model of the Christian life and growth goals for group participants
- A teaching style with which group members can identify

2. DEVELOP A "PROSPECT LIST"

Who are the people, by name, who might participate in a new group?

3. IDENTIFY THE TARGET GROUP

Determine the needs and interests of the people you believe would benefit from participation in a group.

4. GET DOWN TO BASICS

- When will the group meet?

- Where will it meet?

- How often will it meet?

- What will it do?

5. PUBLICIZE THE NEW GROUP

- Make visitation personal.
- Communicate more than once.
- Focus on the benefits of participation.

6. PRAY

- For potential participants
- For the guidance of the Holy Spirit

PROMOTING YOUR GROUP

OBJECTIVE: Design a small-group promotional plan.

TIME: Five minutes (sub-group time).

PROCESS:

1. Promoting can be the most exciting part of starting a group. You have done all the preparatory work; now have fun, meet new people, and study God's Word.

2. Have each sub-group come up with three promotional ideas.

3. Have a volunteer record ideas from all the groups on a flip chart. Have participants write the ideas they would use in their manual.

4. After you have created the flip chart list, you may want to add ideas from the following list.

   ◆ Choose a special name for your small group.
   ◆ Design a logo to identify your group, and use it on all literature.
   ◆ Use flyers and brochures to inform people about your group.
   ◆ Use the church bulletin and newsletter to keep your congregation informed about this ministry, giving updates, listing new groups, leadership training dates, and other details.
   ◆ Talk about your group at every opportunity.
   ◆ After sending personal invitations, divide the list of prospects and make personal follow-up calls.
   ◆ Provide a box to check on worship service visitors cards for those who would be interested in attending a small group.
   ◆ Offer babysitting for children of group members.
   ◆ Use personal testimonies in the church services, in Sunday school, or wherever it is appropriate to talk about your group.
   ◆ After the group has begun, encourage all its members to bring friends.
   ◆ Use visuals, such as balloons to promote parental support groups (send home with children), buttons with a small-group logo, or stickers to go on permanent name tags.
   ◆ When you begin the small-group ministry, use a mock living room setting in the church's main foyer to demonstrate a small-group Bible study. Have a sign-up booth nearby.
   ◆ During one of your services, probably Wednesday night, break the congregation into small groups for prayer and fellowship, to experience the small-group approach.
   ◆ Ask your pastor to preach on small groups.

5. In ongoing training sessions with your leadership, emphasize the importance of developing new promotional ideas.

   ◆ New members—If you include a presentation on groups when you welcome new members to your congregation, offer two different thrusts, one for enlistment, and another for training. Allow anyone to attend training, but do not push people into leadership. Some may want to attend more than one training session before they are ready. Some churches put new members into small groups at the end of the orientation sessions.

PROMOTING YOUR GROUP

Record your promotional ideas.

1.

2.

3.

4.

5.

6.

ELEPHANT FLYER

OBJECTIVE: Design an effective flyer.

TIME: Will vary.

PROCESS: Review the "Elephant Flyer."

Encourage creativity in promoting groups. The "Elephant Flyer" on page 143 was printed on pink paper and created quite a stir! On any flyer you use, include all the information needed, including a map. Notice that this flyer gives the tentative schedule and leaves no doubt about the length of the study. This is very important for people with busy lives.

SINGLE'S FORUM — BIBLE STUDY
Please come study and fellowship with us!

WHEN
Every Tuesday night, 7:30–9:00 PM
For 1 hour Bible study/discussion, then prayer and sharing

Come early for iced tea and to meet everyone!

HOSTESS
Brenda Williams

WHERE
2535 Monaco Lane
Carrollton
Work: 555-5111
Home: 555-2766

LEADER
Gene Madison

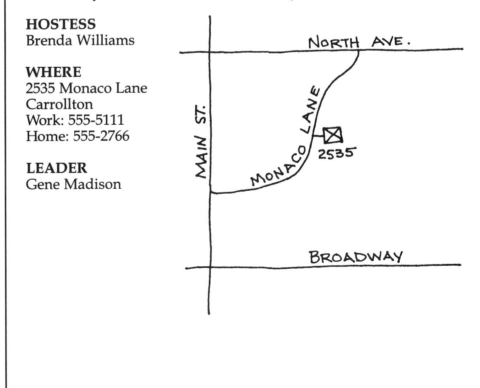

COMMUNITY FLYER

OBJECTIVE: Understand the components of a good flyer.

TIME: Will vary.

PROCESS: Review the "Community Flyer."

On this "Community Flyer," there is an attempt to keep the creative from looking too churchy, which can make unchurched people shy away. Rather, make an appeal for friendship, using terms like "friendly," "exciting," and "join us."

CHRISTIAN REFORMED CHURCH

COMMUNITY CALLER

Donaldson at Elmdale   Church telephone: 563-1031
Joel R. Becker, Pastor

COMING THIS FALL!

FRIENDLY AND EXCITING WAYS TO DISCOVER YOUR BIBLE

You and a friend are invited to attend an interfaith Bible study. We offer opportunities for men, women, and children to participate in fellowship and organized Bible study groups. No previous knowledge or experience necessary!

COME AND JOIN US

71

COFFEE BREAK EVANGELISM FLYER

OBJECTIVE: Understand the components of an effective flyer.

TIME: Will vary.

PROCESS: Review the "Coffee Break Evangelism Flyer."

In this discover your Bible flyer, several women are shown discussing the Bible. This flyer gives many details. First, it mentions an interfaith Bible study for all women. Then it promotes meeting new people in a caring fellowship. In neighborhoods today, people are seeking this fellowship. They want to reach out, but you must reach out to them.

Notice two more important points:

♦ Child care is not only provided, but includes a story hour.
♦ "No previous knowledge or experience expected" is printed on the flyer.

SMALL-GROUP LIST

OBJECTIVE: Design a promotional list of small groups.

TIME: Will vary.

PROCESS: Review the small-group list.

Promoting your groups to church members and community is vital. The "Small-Group List" shown on page 149 provides all the necessary pieces of information necessary for someone to visit a group. It may take several visits before a person settles on one group. The list allows people to quickly check zip codes, street addresses, day and time of meeting, and any other pertinent details, such as child care, women-only groups, and singles. This list should be available at your church information desk, in the library, and by mail on request. It can also be used by visitation teams when visiting prospects.

This listing helps to show where you are in the ministry, and from time to time it should be printed in your church newsletter.

In a brochure on groups, a special group code would refer to support groups, parental groups, cancer support groups, divorce recovery groups, older adult groups, and others.

SMALL-GROUP LIST

INJOY CIRCLE GROUPS

ZIP CODE	HOSTESS/LEADER	MEETING LOCATION	PHONE	DAY	TIME	CODE
75002	Tucker/Tucker	15 Gettisburg, Dallas	576-5981	T	7:00-9:00 PM	SP
75006	Washington/Moore	413 Roaring Springs Dr., Allendon	574-0319	T	7:00-9:00 PM	W
75007	Kulp/Armstrong	2535 Melissa, Franklin	635-4080	Th	7:30-9:30 PM	MS
75007	Foy/Foy	1820 Peters Cn. #4407, Franklin	630-8371	M	7:00-9:00 PM	M
75007	Patrick/Patrick	2330 Castle Rock Rd., Franklin	574-9766	Th	7:00-9:00 PM	W
75010	Adderley/Shelton	2018 Lorient, Franklin	528-1536	T	7:30-9:30 PM	C
75024	Owens/Hall	2006 La Vaca Tr., Franklin	574-5384	F	7:00-9:00 PM	SP
75040	Cennamer/Cennamer	4608 Charles Pl., Palmer	632-8014	T	10:00-11:15 AM	W*
75042	Fortner/Reynolds	1310 Paris Dr., Littleton	531-5357	M	7:30-9:30 PM	W
75042	Sloan/Davis	2436 Richview Ct., Littleton	473-4837	T	9:00-11:00 AM	W*
75075	Hatfield/Logan	2709 Big Oaks, Littleton	632-5952	TH	7:30-8:30 PM	M
75075	Marshall/Marshall	5328 Seascape Ln., Palmer	382-5436	M	12:30-2:00 PM	C
75075	Prizer/Young	1013 Valley Creek, Dr., Palmer	382-7281	T	7:30-9:30 PM	MS
75075	Young/Buroker	1328 Watersedge Dr., Palmer	382-7098	M	7:30-9:00 PM	BW
75080	Barnett/Eliott	3101 Winchester Dr., Palmer	636-3419	Th	7:30-9:00 PM	M

Codes

BW = Business Women
C = Couples
M = Men Only

MS = Mixed Singles
SP = Special
W = Women Only
* = Child Care Available

HOMECOMING CARD

OBJECTIVE: Describe one use of written communication.

TIME: Will vary.

PROCESS: Review the "Homecoming Card."

When groups break, for any reason, it is difficult to pull the members back together. Using a creative theme, such as "homecoming," may work for you. It gives everyone permission to return, no strings attached.

Be sure you have name tags at this meeting!

HOMECOMING CARD

IT'S HOMECOMING AT YOUR INJOY CIRCLE!
Our Injoy group is celebrating HOMECOMING for its members and visitors during January, on Tuesday, January 5 and 19, at 7:30 p.m.

Please reserve these times on your calendar and come join us for fellowship and Bible study.

James and Martha Bennett
1033 Valley View Road
Glen Place, TX 75240
555-6612

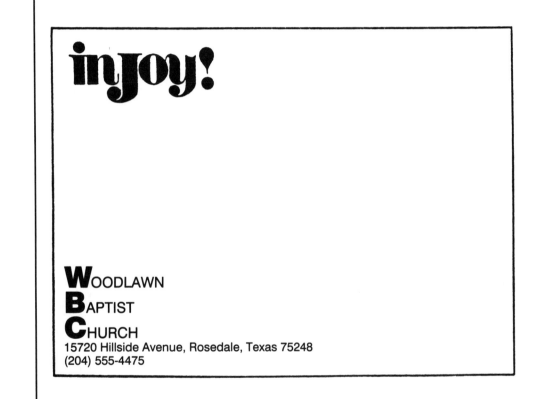

SMALL-GROUP OBSERVATION

OBJECTIVE: Understand the make-up of a healthy group.

TIME: Will vary.

PROCESS:

1. Once you have been trained in leading a small group, it is helpful to observe an existing group.

2. Arrange to visit an existing group. If you have no true small-group Bible studies, visit a Sunday school class or a training class.

3. Respond to each question or statement on the form on pages 153-154. Make notes if you would have done things differently.

4. At your first regular leadership meeting following training, bring these sheets for a review.

SMALL-GROUP OBSERVATION

1. How did the leader introduce the lesson?

2. How did the leader establish rapport with the group?

3. Describe how the leader guided the discussion.

4. Was there an assistant leader? If so, what role did he or she play?

5. How did the leader field questions?

6. Did the leader use questions to draw out group members?

75

7. What techniques did the leader use to keep the discussion clear?

8. Did the leader change from "guide" to "teacher"? If "yes," why?

9. Describe the group prayer time.

10. How would you describe the atmosphere, and how was it affected by the leader?

11. Critique the schedule: Did the group start and stop on time; when were refreshments served; when were the prayer and share times?

LEADERSHIP HANDBOOK

DEVELOPING A LEADERSHIP HANDBOOK

The leadership handbook is designed to help supervise the coordination and ongoing administration of groups. It should facilitate communication with the coordinator and allow feedback to the coordinator. It positions groups within the total church framework, and helps group leaders do their best. It connects group leaders and the church coordinator. Since church settings vary, leadership handbooks will vary in content. Control of small groups depends on the type of authority placed over the group system, and that is beyond the scope of this manual.

A three-ring binder makes it possible to add to the handbook as the ministry develops. The handbook should have tabs for each section. There are many possible sections that can be tabbed. Include only those that apply to your particular small-group ministry; for example, a list and descriptions of church ministries, calendars, leadership, membership roster, report forms, ongoing training notes, evangelism/outreach, prayer, and key Scriptures.

The following sections in this trainer's manual might be included in a handbook. Take what is given, alter the forms, and write your own philosophy. Make your handbook specific to your purposes.

Create a logo for your small-group ministry, and use it consistently in all printed and promotional materials. (An example is shown.)

PRELIMINARY HANDBOOK PAGES

◆ A letter from your pastor.
  Small groups must incorporate with other programs and ministries in order to be a vital part of the church. The visible and verbal support of the pastor is the lifeline of groups.

◆ A description of the name of your ministry and its significance.

◆ A list of Scriptures that offer biblical support for small groups.

◆ A list of priorities for small groups at your church.
  This list will be prepared by the senior pastor and small-group coordinator, and reviewed and adopted by the small-group steering committee.

◆ A description of the small-group ministry's relationship to the church.
  This description will help the congregation understand the need for and purpose of small groups.

A MESSAGE FROM OUR PASTOR

I thank God for you and your commitment to your small group. You have begun what could become the most meaningful ministry of your life.

Small Bible study groups are not a new concept at our church. When we began, there were many meetings in homes for prayer and Bible study, and through the years both my wife and I have led and participated in several Bible study groups. Each Sunday I see people throughout the congregation who have accepted Christ as their Savior as a result of involvement in a small group, and many of those people are now involved in leadership.

In fact, the beginning of every Christian religious movement can be traced to Bible study groups. These groups have a firm biblical basis and are often referred to in Scripture. They have met in homes, in secret places, even when persecution threatened their existence.

The design and purpose of each small group is two-fold: to reach those who would not readily come to church to hear the gospel preached, and to offer Christ-centered encouragement, truth, and love in their communities.

I am excited. God's hand is directing us in this new endeavor. And His hand also rests on you—to guide you, empower you, and help you offer love to all those you encounter.

May His richest blessings be yours.

INJOY GROUPS
Approach/Method

Interaction

- with God through prayer and discussion of His Word;
- with each other through fellowship, prayer, and study;
- with the unchurched, as friends and acquaintances are invited to participate.

Focus

Need-orientation

- the need to know God and His Word better;
- the need for closer relationships with one another;
- the need for prayer for the difficulties of our lives;
- the need to reach the unchurched for our Lord.

Source

Jesus Christ

- the Person at the center of all we do and say;
- the Person we strive to be near;
- the Person we grow up to be like—together.

Activities

Outreach

- to glorify God, through worship, prayer, and discussion of His Word;
- to the lost, through building relationships and through prayer.

Results

Yielding

- our actions to the principles in God's Word;
- our attention to our relationships with one another;
- our prayers and love to the unchurched.

SCRIPTURAL FOUNDATIONS FOR SMALL GROUPS

We are a "priesthood of believers" directed to:	1 Peter 2:5 Revelation 1:6
Love God and love one another.	Matthew 22:37-39
Continually abide in the teachings of His Word.	John 15:4,7-10
Apply God's truths to our daily lives.	Matthew 7:24-27 James 1:22
Bring the lost into His Kingdom.	Matthew 28:19-20 Acts 1:8
Christ, our primary example, went into homes to minister to small groups of people.	Matthew 8:14-15 Mark 2:1-5 Mark 2:15-17 Luke 8:51-56
Christ sent the Twelve and the Seventy into homes in towns and villages.	Matthew 10:5-13 Luke 10:1-7

In Acts believers worshiped and were taught in their home.	Acts 2:46
	     5:42
	   10:1-48
	   16:25-34,40
	   20:17-20
	   28:30-31

New Testament Christians continued to meet in homes for worship, study, discipleship, and fellowship.	Romans 16:5 1 Corinthians 16:19 Colossians 4:15 Philemon 2

THE PASTOR'S VISION FOR SMALL GROUPS

Evangelism

The small-group ministry will be a people-oriented minority with an evangelistic thrust, reaching the unsaved who are intimidated by a church environment.

Sharing Personal Needs

This ministry will be a place where genuine love and warmth allows for honest interaction and the sharing of deep personal needs, followed by prayer for the hurting areas of wounded lives.

Biblical Knowledge

Gathering in small groups will give opportunity to study God's Word; to interact, discuss, and ask questions; to learn how to apply Scripture to daily living.

Ministry and Service

The small groups will be a place for people to serve and minister to one another.

Christian Fellowship

These groups will encourage Christian fellowship.

THE RELATIONSHIP OF SMALL GROUPS TO SUNDAY SCHOOL AND WORSHIP SERVICES

The Role of the Worship Services

Ministry to the congregation. The worship services are primarily a time of worship, instruction, fellowship, and prayer.

The Role of the Sunday School

Ministry to the community. Sunday school is primarily a time of application-oriented Bible study. Sunday school engages in ministry and outreach through various divisions, departments, and classes.

The Role of the Small Group

Ministry in the community. The small group is primarily a time of fellowship, prayer, Bible study, personal sharing of needs, and evangelism within neighborhoods. The small group provides an exciting local dimension of ministry.

OPTIONAL HANDBOOK PAGES

CHURCH MINISTRIES (tab)

Church Information

After meetings, visitors and new members may wish to ask questions. Church information reference material will help leaders respond from an understanding of church structure, and not have to get back to people who ask about the church. If this information is available, it should be included as a section in the leadership notebook. These are some areas of ministry you could define or describe. A few descriptions are given as samples.

Church worship schedules

Sunday school departments

Children's department

Senior adults

Median adults

Single adults

Sunday school class locations

Young married adults

Youth department

Bus ministry

Deaf ministry

Discovery class

Food closet

Hospital visitation

Media ministries

Library/bookstore

Music department

Pastoral counseling

Men's ministry

Women's ministry

Special education

Volunteer department

Wedding coordinator

Youth Department

Youth activities involve a full calendar of monthly events aimed at meeting the needs of young people, grades seven through twelve. Sunday school classes meet at 9:00 a.m. or 10:45 a.m. Sunday evenings begin with senior high choir practice at 4:30 p.m. While the second choir is practicing, the senior high group can attend special church training activity called "Young-A-Versity." "Heartbeat," a time of fellowship and worship, is offered on Wednesday nights.

Several youth socials are held each month during the school year, and even more events for fun and fellowship take place in the summer. For information, contact [name], minister of youth, at [phone number].

Bus Ministry
Each week the bus ministry reaches people from ten to fifteen nationalities and language groups. All riders are contacted weekly by bus teams, brought to church on Sundays, and invited to monthly planned activities, including picnics, skating, and pizza parties. This ministry requires the commitment of people who can drive, do mechanical work, visit, help on the buses, take younger children to class, teach in Sunday school, work in worship services, and help in the special monthly activities. For information contact [name, bus ministry, phone number].

Deaf Ministry
The deaf ministry Bible study fellowship meets during the early Sunday school (for all ages) in [room number]. During the morning and evening worship services an interpreter signs the service for the deaf. This is at the left front section of the auditorium.

Hospital Visitation
In an intensive hospital visitation program, the pastors, deacons, and church members visit hospitals each day. To report people in the hospital who would like to be visited, call the hospital report number, [phone number].

Media Ministries
Media ministries are responsible for the production and distribution of audio cassettes and related materials to support the church's outreach and training activities. These materials include the pastor's messages, Wednesday Bible studies, pastor's sermons aired on local television, and special staff projects. For information contact [name, phone number].

CALENDARS (tab)
Monthly calendars can be included in this section to provide information about all church activities as well as small-group activities. This helps leaders set priorities and coordinate activities.

A sample small-group calendar follows.

Leadership Meeting Third Wednesday of Each Month 6:00-7:00 p.m.

January 18   (Wednesday)

February 15   (Wednesday)

March 15   (Wednesday)

April 19   (Wednesday)

May 17   (Wednesday)

June 21   (Wednesday)

July 29   (Saturday—fellowship)

August 16   (Wednesday)

September 20   (Wednesday)

October 7   (Saturday—all-day retreat)

November 15   (Wednesday)

December 10   (Sunday—fellowship after church)

Leadership Training Schedule

January 13 and 14   (Friday 6:30–9:30 p.m.)
                         (Saturday 8:30 a.m.–3:30 p.m.)

January 25 and 26   (Wednesday/Thursday 9:00 a.m.–2:00 p.m.)

May 5 and 6   (Friday 6:30–9:30 p.m.)
                         (Saturday 8:30 a.m.–3:30 p.m.)

August 25 and 26   (Friday 6:30–9:30 p.m.)
                         (Saturday 8:30 a.m.–3:30 p.m.)

September 13 and 14   (Wednesday/Thursday 9:00 a.m.–2:00 p.m.)

LEADERSHIP (tab)

Leadership in a small group requires the skills of a facilitator and delegator. There are many possible roles for group members to play, and it is the responsibility of the leader to identify gifts and place people in those roles. By doing this, the leader helps group members claim ownership of their small group.

As the leader, *do not do any job someone else can do*—pass out the pie!

The following pages provide a leadership team chart and job descriptions for seven identified roles. Rewrite these job descriptions to fit your own philosophy and church community. You are not limited to this list. Filling the positions will take time, but will enable the leader to get acquainted with group members.

As you fill the roles, photocopy your job descriptions and review each one with the person enlisted to do the job, retaining your original copy for future use.

One key position is the assistant leader, who fills in when the leader is absent. Begin immediately to give attention, guidance, and opportunities to lead to the assistant leader, preparing him or her for starting a new group. Also, recommend that potential leaders attend leadership training.

It will be the leader's responsibility to regularly contact each one on the leadership team, encouraging and building them up in their chosen role, and praying for each of them. The leadership team roster on page 175 may help with this responsibility. Complete the form and keep it in your notebook. Send cards on birthdays and anniversaries. This roster will also help you keep aware when a job is vacant and needs to be filled.

With your team, decide on the format you will follow for the group. A suggested meeting format (page 173) and tentative format worksheet (page 174) will allow you to arrange the group meeting to meet your specific needs and requirements. Be flexible; if you see changes need to be made, make them. For example, if you place prayer time at the beginning of the meeting and it takes too much time and hinders Bible study, move prayer to the end.

The last and most important leadership duty will be to establish a team creed (page 176).

When a group is being formed, the first positions to be filled are those of discussion leader, assistant leader, and host or hostess. It is crucial that those initial leaders then develop others within the group to fill the remaining positions.

Responsibilities of the Discussion Leader

1. Attend the monthly training session.

2. Reflect overall vision and priorities for the group.

3. Meet with team leaders for fifteen or twenty minutes before the meeting for prayer and discussion.

4. Oversee coordination of the worship, prayer, sharing, and fellowship in the small-group meeting, in cooperation with others on the leadership team.

a. Worship

   1) Select songs and choruses.

   2) Have songsheets prepared for distribution.

   3) Coordinate musical accompaniment.

b. Prayer

   1) Direct prayer during the meeting.

   2) Pray for your group's target family, your community, and your mission project.

   3) Keep written record of significant prayer requests in the prayer section of your notebook.

   4) Activate a prayer chain within the group.

c. Introduce newcomers

d. Direct sharing of prayer requests and testimonies.

e. Announcements

5. Conduct a weekly small-group home meeting with an appointed host or hostess, and lead in the discussion of the Bible study material.

6. Be responsible, with an assistant leader or secretary, for completing and submitting a written monthly report, a monthly evangelism/outreach report, and for calling in weekly attendance to the small-group coordinator.

7. With the aid of an assistant leader or secretary, call the following people, and record the calls in a telephone diary.

a. Visitors

   1) Thank them for their participation.

   2) Invite them to the upcoming meeting, being certain to specify date, time, and location.

   3) Pray with them concerning any needs or difficulties they might have.

b. New believers

   1) Rejoice with them in their crucial decision.

   2) Give guidelines on daily Bible reading, prayer, and facing difficulties with a Christlike attitude.

   3) Invite them to the next small-group meeting and, if unchurched, to attend your church.

   4) Pray with them, that God would give wisdom, guidance, and provision for all needs.

c. Absent members

   1) Let them know that they were missed.

   2) Ask about needs or problems you or the group could pray about.

   3) Encourage them to participate in the next meeting, making certain to designate date, time, and place.

d. Persons with pronounced needs

   1) Let them know that their needs are remembered and pray with them on the phone.

   2) Encourage them to come to the next meeting and to remain strong in their Christian walk.

8. Accountability to pastor and church leadership.

Responsibilities of the Host or Hostess

1. Make his or her home available for small-group weekly meetings for a period of three to six months.

2. Coordinate light refreshments at the beginning or end of the meeting. The host or hostess is either responsible for providing the refreshments, or for designating another person to bring the refreshments. Refreshments should be light and inexpensive.

3. Meet with others on the leadership team before the meeting for prayer and discussion.

4. Enthusiastically greet those who arrive, making them feel welcome. Discover as much about each person as possible, in order to:

   a. Introduce new people to the discussion leader and other participants.

   b. Relay information to the records secretary or assistant leader.

5. Cooperate with the discussion leader and others on the leadership team, to ensure a smooth flow in the meetings, and participate in the small-group meetings.

6. Attend the monthly training session.

Responsibilities of the Assistant Discussion Leader

1. Meet with those on the leadership team fifteen to twenty minutes before the meeting for prayer and discussion.

2. Spearhead the evangelistic thrust of the group.

   a. Make a report of outreach activities during the group meeting.

   b. Designate an unsaved target person or target family to pray for and reach out to each month.

   c. Write a missionary on a foreign field each month, praying in the group for him and his family.

   d. Canvass the neighborhood annually, in a house-to-house community saturation strategy, inviting others to the group. (This is done best in teams of two or three.)

3. Assist the discussion leader by calling on and compiling written records of the following categories of people:

   - Visitors
   - New believers
   - Absent members
   - People with pronounced needs
   - Regular members

4. Substitute for the discussion leader or direct specified activities.

5. Assist the discussion leader and secretary in updating information on the small-group participant information form on page 181.

Responsibilities of the Records Secretary/Follow-up Coordinator

1. Meet with those on the leadership team for fifteen to twenty minutes before the meeting, for prayer and discussion.

2. Complete a small-group participant information form (page 181) on those who attend small-group meetings, including this information about each individual:

   a. Name in full.

   b. Home and mailing addresses.

   c. Home and work telephone numbers.

   d. Occupation.

   e. Date of birth.

   f. Wedding anniversary.

   g. List of family members, with their names and ages.

   h. Record of times called or visited.

   i. Any outstanding needs or difficulties.

3. Assist the discussion leader by completing and turning in written and verbal reports to the small-group coordinator.

4. Make personal calls to visitors, new believers, absent members, and persons with needs, and compile a written record of those calls on the information sheets. Refer to the list of steps under item 7 on pages 168-169.

5. Distribute copies of needed materials to all participants.

Responsibilities of the Worship/Prayer Leader

1. Meet with others on the leadership team for fifteen to twenty minutes before the meeting for prayer and discussion.

2. Select two or three choruses or songs and be responsible to coordinate musical accompaniment before the meeting.

3. Mingle with participants and help them enjoy the refreshments, and then guide in transition to the time of worship, usually through an announcement.

4. Have new people introduced.

5. Open the worship portion of the meeting, through a time of song, prayer, and brief testimony. It is advisable to record prayer requests and to choose a designated prayer leader.

6. Direct prayer.

   a. Pray yourself.

   b. Designate others to pray.

   c. Direct the groups on how to pray. This might also include recording prayer requests or praise reports of answered prayer. Remember to pray for your group's target family, your community, and your mission project.

7. Record significant prayer requests, including:

   a. Date.

   b. Name of person making request.

   c. Nature of request made.

   d. Telephone number of person making request.

   e. Praise report of answered prayer. By keeping a written record of a request, the prayer leader can know to ask what happened in that area the next time the group meets. Moreover, the giving of the praise reports for answered prayer builds the faith of the group.

8. Introduce the small-group discussion leader, and help make the transition from worship to Bible study.

9. Make sure announcements are made at the beginning or end of the meeting, and that either the leader or another person closes the meeting in prayer.

10. Activate a prayer chain within the group, connect with prayer chains in other groups, and coordinate prayer needs at times other than the meetings.

11. Take a wide variety of approaches in prayer, such as circle prayer, directed prayer, conversational prayer, the five-finger prayer, and praying through the newspaper (see page 184). Be creative.

12. Coordinate with the assistant leader to give prayer its proper priority.

Responsibilities of Children's Coordinator
1. Attend designated training sessions supervised by the leadership of the church children's department.

2. Supervise children taken to church or another place for child care, or supervise children taught in either another portion of the same house or a different home during the adult group meeting.

3. Serve as a liaison between the group and child care needs. Secure a sitter or appoint one from within the group, or coordinate use of the church nursery facilities. Teach the children's group, using Bible stories, prayer, crafts, and activities.

4. Work with the assistant leader or records secretary in including information about the children on the small-group participant information form (page 181) and written report.

5. Make personal calls to children who are visitors, new believers, absent members, and have pronounced needs, as well as phoning parents with any pertinent information.

6. Make announcements in the adult group concerning important information on the children's group or child care.

Responsibilities of the Greeter
1. Arrive early for each small-group meeting, in order to assist the host or hostess in greeting participants.

2. See that all members and visitors wear name tags.

3. Enthusiastically and warmly welcome everyone at the door.

4. Introduce new participants to the group, and help everyone comfortably mingle during refreshments.

5. Find out information on any new individuals, and channel this information to the assistant leader or records secretary.

6. Make certain each new person is introduced to the group in the meeting time. This task is primarily the worship leader's, but he or she might delegate it to the greeters, or might forget to mention a name that the greeter would recall.

Suggested Meeting Format

6:30-7:00 p.m. Team prayer. Those in the smalll-group leadership team arrive early for prayer and discussion.

7:00 Greet participants. Greeters welcome arriving participants, introduce them to the discussion leader and others, and hand out name tags. Refreshments can be made available at this time or at the conclusion. All are encouraged to talk and fellowship.

7:20-7:30 Meeting begins. The worship leader or discussion leader gathers everyone in the designated room.

7:30-7:45 Prayer and worship. The worship leader directs the group in prayer and song, and possibly testimonies.

7:45-8:30 Bible study. Interaction is a vital key and should be the goal of every discussion leader.

8:30-9:00 Prayer, ministry, and fellowship. Time for prayer and ministry to the needs of those present, possibly followed by refreshments and fellowship.

9:00 Conclusion. The group meeting is concluded. Members may linger for a few minutes.

TENTATIVE MEETING FORMAT WORKSHEET

Activity	Estimated Time	Person Responsible
Prayer prior to meeting		
Greet arriving participants		
Refreshments and fellowship		
Meeting formally begins		
Announcements		
Introduce newcomers		
Testimonies		
Opening prayer time		
Worship and song		
Lead Bible study discussion		
Prayer time		
Refreshments		

LEADERSHIP TEAM

Discussion Leader: _____

    Address: _____

Telephone number: _____

    Birthday: _____ Wedding anniversary: _____

Host/Hostess: _____

    Address: _____

Telephone number: _____

    Birthday: _____ Wedding anniversary: _____

Assistant Leader: _____

    Address: _____

Telephone number: _____

    Birthday: _____ Wedding anniversary: _____

Secretary/Follow-Up Coordinator: _____

    Address: _____

Telephone number: _____

    Birthday: _____ Wedding anniversary: _____

Worship/Prayer Leader: _____

    Address: _____

Telephone number: _____

    Birthday: _____ Wedding anniversary: _____

Children's Coordinator: _____

    Address: _____

Telephone number: _____

    Birthday: _____ Wedding anniversary: _____

Greeter: _____

    Address: _____

Telephone number: _____

    Birthday: _____ Wedding anniversary: _____

Leadership Team Creed

1. I will read my Bible daily and take time to develop a growing personal relationship with the Lord Jesus Christ.

2. I will continuously look for the spiritually lost and needy, and enthusiastically lead others to our Lord Jesus Christ.

3. I will pray daily for the unsaved in my community, the needs of those in my small group, the leadership at my church, and upcoming meetings and activities.

4. I will lead those in my group from a position of being served to serving others and work in full cooperation with the leadership team.

5. I will be available to minister to others both during and between meetings.

6. I will be faithful to my home and family and be the person God intended me to be.

7. I will be faithful in my attendance to my church and will be a consistent steward of my tithes and offerings.

8. I will diligently and faithfully fulfill my responsibilities as a member of the leadership team and will keep all confidences shared with me by participants in the group.

9. I will be positive in my attitude and speech, not criticizing, while actively affirming the worth of each individual by my upbuilding words and actions.

10. I will be honest and open in my relationship with God and with my group, ever keeping in mind the importance of "speaking the truth in love" (Ephesians 4:15).

REPORT FORMS (tab)

Accountability to the small-group coordinator is a commitment which must be made by each member of group leadership. One way to demonstrate accountability is through written reports.

Properly executed forms can help you organize and coordinate groups. Many decisions about the ministry are based on statistical data gathered from the reports. Two major areas affected are budgeting and curriculum.

Budgeting for a small-group ministry should be supported with substantial documentation on attendance. As groups grow in number and their needs become more diverse, the budget should increase to accommodate this growth. Some materials and programs affected by reporting include the number of training manuals needed, training sessions offered, a yearly recognition and awards day, retreats, monthly or weekly meeting costs, and curriculum needs.

Reports help gauge the number of copies of curriculum that are needed. If your church writes its own curriculum, accurate numbers are necessary for reproducing it, and if you purchase your curriculum, that count is equally important.

The following six report forms serve different purposes.

Small-Group Enrollment Roster

The group enrollment roster is used to check weekly attendance. The leader or secretary will tally the information, then call in the report to the coordinator, who will include it with other church numerical reports. This information should be used to follow up absent members.

Small-Group Monthly Report

Using the information recorded on the enrollment roster, the secretary will submit a monthly small-group report to the group coordinator. If you want to have a weekly group report, simply re-title the form. Monthly reports are usually more acceptable to group leadership and still serve the needs of the coordinator.

Small-Group Participant Information Form

The small-group participant information form is designed for small-group leaders. It can be expanded as a leader gets better acquainted with the participants. One way is to pass out an index card and request bits of information from time to time. Another is to build an opening sharing question around pieces of the information, record responses, and then transfer the information after a meeting. (Never pass this sheet out to have it completed!) When you call to check on members, this form allows you to recall dates, children's names, and important things going on in group members' lives, as well as pray for specific needs.

Monthly Evangelism/Outreach Report

This information will help make you aware of each group's efforts in the areas of prayer, outreach, missions, and testimonies, as well as questions that should be addressed by the small-group coordinator.

Telephone Diary

The telephone diary will keep track of telephone calls to members, visitors, new Christians, absent persons or those with prayer requests. Record the date of call, the name of the person called, his or her phone number, the reason for the call, the response, a date for the next call, and follow-up action. This one procedure will help leaders become more caring, more aware of needs, and more responsible for those God has put under their care.

As small-group coordinator, you should keep your own telephone diary of calls made to leadership. Your caring touch and your prayers and encouragement to leadership will model what you want them to do for their members. This is the life line to successful small-group systems.

Participant Placement Form

There is no consensus among group coordinators as to whether participants should or should not be assigned to groups. It works in some churches and does not work in others. One form that works well for participant placement is a three-part NCR form, color-coded white, yellow, and blue. The white copy goes to the group the person has been assigned to, the yellow copy goes to the visitor, and the blue copy goes to the small-group coordinator. This three-part form provides:

1. Participants with the name, address, and phone number of the group they are to visit.

2. Group leaders with potential participants' names, addresses, and phone numbers, so they can call and extend personal invitations.

3. Group coordinators with enough information to make sure the visits were made and to see if additional information or help is needed.

SMALL-GROUP ENROLLMENT ROSTER

Discussion Leader: _____

Secretary: _____

Name	Dates																
Total members																	
Total visitors																	
Total																	

(M) Member   (*) Visitor   (A) Absent

SMALL-GROUP MONTHLY REPORT

Discussion Leader: _____

Secretary: _____

Date: _____ Leader's phone: _____

Small-Group Members	Small-Group Visitors
Total members	Total visitors

Average Attendance _____

SMALL-GROUP PARTICIPANT INFORMATION FORM

Name: _____

Address: _____

City: _____ State: _____ Zip code: _____

Home phone: _____ Work phone: _____

Occupation: _____

Birthdate: _____ Wedding anniversary: _____

Family Information			
Name	Relationship	Birthday	Occupation

Times called or visited:

History of outstanding needs:

Additional comments:

MONTHLY EVANGELISM/OUTREACH REPORT

Discussion Leader: _____

Secretary: _____

Date: _____ Leader's phone: _____

Prayer: At each meeting we have been praying for the unsaved and unchurched in our community.

☐ Yes   ☐ No

Target family:

Name: _____

Address: _____

Any particular needs: _____

Neighborhood canvassing:

Date: _____

Results: _____

_____

Mission project:

Comments/suggestions:

Reports/testimonies:

Submitted by: _____

TELEPHONE DIARY

Date	Name	Phone Number	Reason Called	Response	Follow-up	Date

PRAYER (tab)

1. Purposes of prayer in the small-group meeting.

   a. To build faith.

   b. To meet needs within the groups.

   c. To enable the group to minister beyond itself to others.

   d. To lead to worship.

   e. To strengthen relationships within the group.

   f. To help model the importance of prayer to the members of the group.

   g. To keep attention directed to the Lord Jesus Christ and off oneself.

2. Plan for prayer. The group may feel the need to pray one or more times at a meeting. Need should determine the amount of time spent. Sometimes Bible reading or study preceding the prayer time helps to set a more productive climate for prayer.

3. Methods of prayer.

   a. Circle prayer: Sitting in a circle, each member has the option of praying aloud.

   b. Conversational prayer: Pray in short sentences, using normal conversational language.

   c. Directed prayer: A person, directed by the leader, intercedes about another's specific prayer request.

   d. Prayer partners: People are paired off to pray together.

   e. Praying through the newspaper: Intercessory prayer for people and events in the news.

   f. Five-finger prayer: Topical conversational prayer in which each finger represents a segment of society. Pray moving from the thumb to the little finger.

4. Focus of prayer.

   a. The unsaved in the community.

   b. Family, friends, and coworkers.

   c. Church leadership.

   d. Past, present, and future concerns.

   "Again, I tell you that if two of you on earth agree about anything you ask for, it will be done for you by my Father in heaven. For where two or three come together in my name, there am I with them." (Matthew 18:19-20, NIV)

   "If you remain in me and my words remain in you, ask whatever you wish, and it will be given you." (John 15:7, NIV)

PRAYER DIARY

Date	Person Requesting Prayer	Phone Number	Nature of Request	Date Answered
1.				
2.				
3.				
4.				
5.				
6.				
7.				
8.				
9.				
10.				
11.				
12.				
13.				
14.				
15.				
16.				
17.				
18.				
19.				
20.				
21.				
22.				
23.				

Prayer Chain Guidelines

1. The daytime prayer chains will begin at 8:00 a.m. The evening chains will begin at 6:00 p.m.

2. Be prepared to receive requests by placing a pen and your notebook request sheet by your phone.

3. Pass the request on immediately to the person below your name on the prayer-chain list. If there is no answer, keep calling down the list until someone is reached so that the chain will not be broken. At a later time try to recall the person(s) you missed to share the request. Do not allow the chain to break.

4. Do not take time to chat. Pass on the requests, then pray before doing anything else. Pray about requests to God; do not pray about the answers you would like. Pray fervently. Keep requests confidential. Pray for the request as long as you feel it is necessary, depending on the nature of the request.

5. The last person called should call the first person on the prayer-chain list, to let him or her know the chain has been completed.

6. Call prayer answers to your prayer leader.

7. Much time will be saved if you advise the person ahead of you on the chain if you are planning to be out of town for any length of time.

The success of the prayer chain depends on each person doing his part.

PRAYER CHAIN LIST

Name	Address	Phone
1.		
2.		
3.		
4.		
5.		
6.		
7.		
8.		
9.		
10.		

NURSERY GUIDELINES FOR SMALL-GROUP MEETINGS

Nursery at the Meeting Site

1. A nursery will be provided for children at the church every Tuesday and Friday morning from 8:45 until noon.

2. The care provided is for children who are three weeks old through kindergarten.

3. A special night nursery will be provided for preschoolers if arranged in advance.

Nursery Held at Another Site

1. Your church will supply nursery workers or volunteers to care for the children of small-group members on Tuesday and Friday mornings.

2. Nursery workers will be in homes to care for children who are three years and older. The children younger than three years old need to go to the regular church nursery because the rooms are better equipped to meet their individual needs.

3. Exceptions will be made *only* if the situation is discussed in advance with the children's minister and small-group coordinator.

JOB DESCRIPTION OF THE SMALL-GROUP COORDINATOR
Purpose and Scope
1. The coordinator, under the general supervision of the pastor, is responsible for the administration of the entire small-group program. This responsibility includes the organization and supervision of all aspects of the program, in cooperation with all other divisions of the church.

2. The coordinator of small groups is expected to be in continuous control of the small-group systems, to communicate effectively with the church congregation (both members and staff), and to be a leader in the field of small groups while serving as the official small-group representative from the church.

Principal Responsibilities
1. Develop policies and procedures to meet immediate and long-range goals of the small-group ministry.

2. Plan, organize, implement, manage, and evaluate the small-group program.

3. Continually analyze and interpret relevant influencing factors, such as the community demographics, levels of development of church membership, and changing needs.

4. Encourage participation of small-group leadership in all areas of the church.

Specific Responsibilities
1. Enlist and train a curriculum committee, which will review all curricula written or purchased, for use by the small groups.

2. Enlist and direct lay area directors who are responsible for a number of groups.

3. Prepare and adhere to a budget.

4. Direct the investigation of new materials for possible use by groups.

5. Direct the development and pilot testing of new types of groups.

6. Identify and enlist small-group leadership, both hosts and leaders.

7. Direct initial and ongoing training of group leadership.

8. Develop a leadership manual to be used in coordination of the small-groups system.

9. Maintain member and visitor attendance records for all groups.

10. Maintain regular contact with leadership to encourage, motivate, and model visitation habits.

Requirements
Salary varies, depending on the level of education and experience.

1. Education.

   Level 1: B.A. degree (any field). Coursework in counseling and adult education helpful, but not mandatory.

   Level 2: Masters in religious education or an equivalent.

Level 3: Ph.D. in adult education or doctorate of religious education.

2. Experience.

Level 1: Experience leading a small group.

Level 2: Lay experience in directing a small-group program.

Level 3: Professional experience in directing a small-group program.

3. All Levels.

A commitment to full-time Christian work.

Note: This sample can be rewritten to meet the needs of a specific church.

SAMPLE SUNDAY BULLETIN COPY

An exciting time of leadership training will prepare you to minister to others.

Training Comments

What one thing do you feel is most effective in this training course?

- ◆ Good literature.
- ◆ Focus on leadership and Christian training.
- ◆ Organized material.
- ◆ Learning conversational prayer techniques.
- ◆ Characteristics of effective leaders.
- ◆ Specific suggestions for dealing with problems.
- ◆ Small-group practice—applying what we are being taught.

Who Is Eligible?

- ◆ Anyone who would like to begin their preparation for leadership.
- ◆ Those waiting to start small groups and needing training.

Benefits

- ◆ Become a better communicator at home, at work, and in your small group.
- ◆ Identify your leadership style and how best to involve others in group participation.
- ◆ Be prepared to reach unsaved friends, family, and coworkers.

Dates

Daytime Training	March 14, 15, 16 from 9:00 a.m. to 2:00 p.m. Lunch included Nursery provided/reservations required
Weekend Training	March 10 from 7:00 to 10:00 p.m. March 11 from 9:00 a.m. to 3:30 p.m. Lunch included Nursery provided/reservations required

Registration

Call [name, number] to make your reservation, or sign below and drop in the collection plate.

Name: _____

Home phone: _____ Work phone: _____

POTENTIAL LEADERSHIP QUESTIONNAIRE

Name: _____

Address: _____

Home phone: _____ Work phone: _____

Date of birth: _____ Place of birth: _____

Personal Background
How long have you lived in this area? _____

Do you work outside your home? ❑ Yes ❑ No

Which are you? ❑ Single ❑ Married ❑ Divorced ❑ Separated ❑ Widowed

Names and ages of your children: _____

_____

_____

Do you and your spouse attend church together? ❑ Yes ❑ No

Do you and your family have devotions together? ❑ Yes ❑ No

Spiritual Beginnings
When did you become a Christian? _____

Give a brief testimony of how and when you came to know Jesus Christ as your personal Lord and Savior.

_____

_____

_____

_____

_____

_____

_____

_____

When were you baptized? _____

Where were you baptized? _____

If someone in your small group asked you how to become a Christian, how would you respond?

_____

_____

_____

_____

_____

_____

_____

Personal Devotions
Do you have a daily quiet time? If so, what does this involve?

_____

_____

_____

_____

Describe what role your own personal Bible study plays in your life.

_____

_____

_____

_____

_____

What do you feel are your greatest strengths in your Christian walk?

_____

_____

_____

What do you feel are your greatest weaknesses in your Christian walk?

_____

_____

_____

Affiliation with This Church
How long have you been attending this church? _____

When did you become a member? _____

Why did you decide to become a member? _____

_____

_____

_____

What ministries have you been involved in since becoming a member? (For example: choir, Sunday school teacher, Bible study leader, deacon, volunteer, bus ministry, etc.)

_____

_____

_____

_____

Past Involvement with Home Groups
Have you previously been involved with home groups?   ❑ Yes   ❑ No

If you answered yes, in what capacity did you serve in a previous home group?

❑ Member   ❑ Leader   ❑ Teacher   ❑ Host/Hostess   ❑ Other

Please give a brief history of previous involvements with home Bible study groups and overall Bible study leader or teacher experience.

_____

_____

_____

_____

_____

_____

Current Interest in Small-Group Ministry
Why do you want to be involved in small-group ministry?

_____

_____

_____

_____

_____

_____

If married, does your spouse support you in this leadership position? ❏ Yes   ❏ No

Why would this be an important consideration? _____

_____

_____

What do you feel your greatest strengths in small-group leadership are?

_____

_____

_____

_____

_____

(As part of your leadership questionnaire, you may want to include your church's doctrinal statement.)

SAMPLE TRAINING EVALUATION FORM

Ministry name: _____   Leadership training: _____

Church: _____   Your name: _____

Address: _____   Instructor: _____

City: _____   State: _____ Zip: _____

Participant, please check this evaluation sheet, as it applies to your experience in the small-group leadership training. Thank You. You do not need to sign this form.

1. Which session have you attended? (Please circle one.)

   Thursday   Friday   Saturday

2. How would you rate this course?

   Excellent ❑   Good ❑   Fair ❑   Poor ❑

3. What one thing do you feel is *most effective* in this course?

4. What one thing do you think has been *least helpful*?

5. Please use E–Excellent, G–Good, F–Fair, and P–Poor to rate the following:

   ___ Room facilities

   ___ Discussion

   ___ Material covered

   ___ Your own participation

   ___ Instructor

   ___ How course was planned

6. Please write in any suggestions or criticisms that you feel would be interesting or helpful.

ONGOING LEADERSHIP TRAINING SAMPLE AGENDA

Leadership Rally Agenda
August 24, 1988

6:00   Opening

6:10   Review of curriculum

6:30   Share and care

7:00   Sanctuary/testimonies

8:00   Outreach strategy

8:30   Brainstorming on groups

POTENTIAL LEADERSHIP LIST

Person	Source of Contact	Response to Leadership
Name:_____ Address:_____ _____ Phone:_____		
Name:_____ Address:_____ _____ Phone:_____		
Name:_____ Address:_____ _____ Phone:_____		
Name:_____ Address:_____ _____ Phone:_____		
Name:_____ Address:_____ _____ Phone:_____		

ATTENDANCE REPORT

Zip Code	Leader / Hostess	Average Attendance 1990	1991	Meeting Location	Phone	Day	Time	Code
1.								
2.								
3.								
4.								
5.								
6.								
7.								
8.								
9.								

Codes

BG = Boys and Girls	ME = Men Only
BW = Business Women	MS = Mixed Singles
C = Couples	SP = Special
	W = Women Only

200

WEEKLY ATTENDANCE, THIRD QUARTER 1991

Zip Code	Leader	7/4	7/11	7/18	7/25	8/1	8/8	8/15	8/22	8/29	9/5	9/12	9/19	9/26
	Total													

SOURCES (for participant pages)

PAGES 12, 45, 51-52
Developed by Karen Hurston.

PAGE 14
Kevin M. Thompson, *Equipping the Saints: A Manual for Small Group Ministry* (Minneapolis, MN: Christians in Action Campus Ministry, 1981).

PAGES 16, 18, 19
First and last items by Roberta Hestenes, *Using the Bible in Groups* (Philadelphia, PA: Westminster Press, 1985).

Other items by John Mallison, *Building Small Groups in the Christian Community* (Australia: Renewal Publications, 1978).

PAGES 17, 25, 27
Roberta Hestenes, *Using the Bible in Groups* (Philadelphia, PA: Westminster Press, 1985).

PAGE 35
Jill Briscoe, adapted from *Faith Enough to Finish* (Wheaton, IL: Victor Books, 1987).

PAGES 46, 47
Wyn Arn and Charles Arn, *The Master's Plan for Making Disciples* (Pasadena, CA: Church Growth Press, 1982). Summarized by Karen Hurston.

PAGE 49
Darrell Robinson, *People Sharing Jesus: Witness and Soul-Winning Seminar*, 1979.

PAGE 54
Taken from *Small Group Leaders' Handbook*, by Ron Nicholas et al. © 1982 by InterVarsity Christian Fellowship of the USA. Used by permission of InterVarsity Press, P.O. Box 1400, Downers Grove, IL 60515.

PAGE 57
How to Lead Small Group Bible Studies (Colorado Springs, CO: NavPress, 1982).

Ideas from Harvey Herman, Chi Alpha Campus Ministry Director, University of Nebraska. Reprinted from *Equipping the Saints: A Manual for Small Group Ministry* by Kevin Thompson.

PAGE 60
How to Lead Small Group Bible Studies (Colorado Springs, CO: NavPress, 1982) and *The Small Group Letter* (NavPress).

PAGES 64-65, 71, 72, 75-76
Coffee Break Evangelism training material (Grand Rapids, MI: Church Development Resources, 1987).

BIBLIOGRAPHY

1. Adler, Ronald B.; Towne, Neil. *Looking Out Looking In*. New York: Holt, Rinehart and Winston, 1984.

2. Barker, Steve; Johnson, Judy; Malone, Rob; Nicholas, Ron; Whallon, Doug. *Good Things Come in Small Groups*. Downers Grove, IL: InterVarsity Press, 1985.

3. Barker, Steve; Johnson, Judy; Long, Jimmy; Malone, Rob; Nicholas, Ron. *Small Group Leaders' Handbook*. Downers Grove, IL: InterVarsity Press, 1982.

4. Cho, Dr. Paul Yonggi; Hostetler, Harold. *Successful Home Cell Groups*. Plainfield, NJ: Logos International, 1981.

5. Dibbert, Michael T.; Wichern, Frank B. *Growth Groups*. Grand Rapids, MI: Zondervan Publishing House, 1985.

6. Egan, Gerard. *Face to Face*. Monterey, CA: Brooks/Cole Publishing Co., 1973.

7. Evans, Louis H., Jr. *Covenant to Care*. Wheaton, IL: Victor Books, 1985.

8. Griffin, Em. *Getting Together*. Downers Grove, IL: InterVarsity Press, 1982.

9. Hadaway, C. Kirk; Wright, Stuart A.; Du Base, Francis M. *Home Cell Groups and House Churches*. Nashville, TN: Broadman Press, 1987.

10. Hestenes, Roberta. *Using the Bible in Groups*. Philadelphia, PA: Westminister Press, 1985.

11. Hyde, Kathy. *Teaching the Bible to Change Lives*. San Bernardino, CA: Here's Life Publishers, Inc., 1984.

12. Mallison, John. *Building Small Groups*. West Ryde, Australia: Renewal Publications, 1983.

13. Mallison, John. *Creative Ideas*. West Ryde, Australia: Renewal Publications, 1983.

14. Mallison, John. *Growing Christians in Small Groups*. Melbourne, Australia: Joint Board of Christian Education, 1989.

15. Navigators. *How to Lead Small Group Bible Studies*. Colorado Springs, CO: NavPress, 1982.

16. O'Halloran SDB, James. *Living Cells*. Maryknoll, NY: Orbis Books, 1984.

17. Peace, Richard. *Small-Group Evangelism*. Downers Grove, IL: InterVarsity Press, 1985.

18. Richards, Lawrence O. *Sixty-nine Ways to Start a Study Group and Keep It Growing*. Grand Rapids, MI: Zondervan Publishing House, 1973.

19. Scheidel, Thomas M.; Crowell, Laura. *Discussing and Deciding*. New York: Macmillan Publishing Co., Inc., 1979.

20. Slocum, Robert E. *Maximum Ministry: How You as a Layperson Can Impact Your World for Christ.* Colorado Springs, CO: NavPress, 1990.

21. Briscoe, Stuart. *Everyday Discipleship for Ordinary People.* Wheaton, IL: Victor Books, 1988.

22. Warren, Richard; Shell, William A. *12 Dynamic Bible Study Methods for Individuals or Groups.* Wheaton, IL: Victor Books, 1985.